the series on school reform

Patricia A. Wasley
Coalition of
Essential Schools

Ann Lieberman
NCREST

SERIES EDITORS

Joseph P. McDonald
Annenberg Institute
for School Reform

This series also incorporates earlier titles in the
Professional Development and Practice Series

HOW IT WORKS—
Inside a School–College Collaboration

Sidney Trubowitz
Paul Longo

FOREWORD BY SEYMOUR B. SARASON

Teachers College, Columbia University
New York and London

Published by Teachers College Press, 1234 Amsterdam Avenue, New York, NY 10027

Library of Congress Cataloging-in-Publication Data

Trubowitz, Sidney.
   How it works : inside a school–college collaboration / Sidney
  Trubowitz, Paul Longo ; with a foreword by Seymour B. Sarason.
     p.   cm. — (The series on school reform)
   Includes bibliographical references (p.   ) and index.
   ISBN 0-8077-3571-X (paper : alk. paper). — ISBN 0-8077-3572-8
  (cloth : alk. paper)
    1. College–school cooperation — United States. I. Longo, Paul.
  II. Title. III. Series.
  LB2331.53.T78   1997
  378.1′03 — dc20
                                      96-32841

ISBN 0-8077-3571-X (paper)
ISBN 0-8077-3572-8 (cloth)

Printed on acid-free paper
Manufactured in the United States of America

04 03 02 01 00 99 98 97   8 7 6 5 4 3 2 1

Contents

Foreword

It is usual in a foreword to commend the book to readers by emphasizing its major significances: issues raised and clarified, new ground broken, scope of inquiry, the theories and practices that will need to be given up or revised, or any other feature that will contribute to the readers' knowledge and that of future investigators. I shall not follow that tradition. This is a very important book that will speak for itself. Let me just say that my enthusiasm for this book is enormous, so much that I take this opportunity to tell the reader certain things about the authors they understandably find difficult to discuss—they allude to them but do not discuss them—but which are absolutely crucial not only for the reader's instruction but for the entire arena of school interventions. I am referring to factors *always* absent in write-ups but *always* present in interventions. I know that what I will say will produce discomfort in Drs. Trubowitz and Longo. It will cause them to blush, to deny they are paragons of a sensitive maturity, to retreat to a stance of unrealistic modesty. They may be sorry they asked me to write this foreword but, having asked me, I know they will keep their word and will include these introductory remarks in this book. And that is part of the story: These are decent people who keep their word, whose values are too personally valuable to be subverted.

Some history about me and this 17-year project: When my dear friend, Saul Cohen, became president of Queens College, one of the first things he did was to take steps to reinvigorate individuals who had taught in and administered public schools before joining the Queens College faculty. To me, this meant that in their striving for professional upward mobility, they had forgotten what it had been like in the trenches.

So I met and began to interact with the authors of this book and their colleagues, always meeting at the middle school with school personnel. Four things became quickly apparent. First, the authors had forgotten nothing about their public school experience. Second, they were *sincerely* respectful of the motivations, anticipations, wariness, and responsibilities of teachers and administrators. Third, they were prepared to learn, accommodate, and to give of themselves in coping with the nitty-gritty problems of school life and organization. Fourth, they had resources they hoped the school would utilize but they knew that it could only happen by developing *over time* a relationship of trust. They proceeded slowly and sensitively, never forgetting who had (and should have) primary responsibility for school policy, goals, and practice.

What I am saying here is that Drs. Trubowitz and Longo are not only wise and smart but extraordinarily decent, likeable people in and out of the school arena. They are the opposite of competitive, arrogant, power hungry, and possess none of the more disconcerting features too often found in professors, for example, bringing "culture" to the Bongo-Bongos. I found it a pleasure, personal and intellectual, to meet with them and so did the school personnel. This is not to say that there were never times when there were disagreements—some surfacing, some not, actions at apparently cross purposes causing frustration and strain, oversights that were not always oversights—and more, but the point when the discontinuation of the collaboration was a possibility was never reached or even approached. When you read this book and ponder the strength of the diverse pressures and unpredictabilities coming from within and without the school, you will appreciate the significance of a collaboration that was mutually rewarding and, wonder of wonders, has continued for almost two decades. It would be both wrong and foolish to attribute all of this to Drs. Trubowitz and Longo, but it is wrong and foolish not to assign them a most crucial role.

I am not describing angels or paragons of virtue. What I am asserting is that these two people are remarkable for possessing a *combination* of personal, intellectual, and experiential assets—without these, those who initiate an ambitious and meaningful school intervention end up disappointed and angry, which is to explain why successful efforts are minuscule in number compared to the failures.

Can you assess the impact of a curriculum independent of who utilizes it? Can you evaluate any form of therapy apart from the therapists who use it? Can you pass judgment, for example, on the usefulness of group learning techniques without taking into account the teachers who employ them? Can you securely say anything about a surgical procedure and leave the surgeons out of the picture?

Similarly, can you accept as valid the accomplishments described in this book without knowing something about Drs. Trubowitz and Longo, things I had opportunity to witness, and requiring me to alter my initial forebodings of failure? As much as anyone in the field, I have observed school interventions. These were not pleasant experiences, however well intentioned and, unlike the story in this book, fiscally well supported. Most were not only failures, but quick ones at that. My experiences are, of course, finite, but in only two cases can I say they were successful. One is in its fifth year in Tucson, spearheaded by Dr. Paul Heckman, with every indication that it will continue. Dr. Heckman is cut from the same cloth as Drs. Trubowitz and Longo. They are amazingly similar in terms of professional experience, personal style, and respect for those whose daily lives are spent in complicated schools in complicated systems, and in their understanding of the brute, inescapable fact that no one wants to change however he or she proclaims the desire to do so.

The track of an atom in a cloud chamber is independent of the personality of the experimenter. How the double helix is formed and works does not require us to say something about the personalities of geneticists. However, in the realm of human relationships and affairs it is a very different ball game. Nowhere is this more obvious than in efforts at educational reform, an area in which replication is literally impossible and where our goal is approximation. In this area even approximation has not been achieved. The reasons are many, but certainly crucially prominent among them has been our inability and/or unwillingness to confront the importance of the kinds of people who attempt to change schools. These are not attempts for which anybody is appropriate, however bright, conscientious, well read, and well intentioned he or she may be. I am passing judgment on no one. I am saying what is obvious: To initiate and sustain a meaningful effort at school change that is personally and intellectually rewarding to all of the participants requires, among other things, a rare combination of personal characteristics.

I trust that the reader now comprehends why I felt compelled to say in this introduction that they cannot truly understand how the story in this book evolved in the absence of what I have tried to say here. I have no doubt that what I have said would be what most (if not all) teachers, administrators, and parents at Louis Armstrong Middle School would say, and what Saul Cohen intuited when he chose the authors of this book to spearhead the project.

This introduction may cause discomfort to the authors. They may not see themselves as I have described them. Even if they did, they could not discuss it forthrightly in the pages that follow — however, I have done so, far less to express my appreciation and wonder for them and their accomplishments and far more to alert the reader to an issue that has gone undiscussed in the literature. And glossing over such a central issue can no longer be tolerated. For too long we have bought and promoted the view that the success of school reform depended on ideas, power or influence, appropriate motivation and commitment, administrative support, and the like. But in the real world of real people nothing is more important than the combination of characteristics possessed by the initiators and implementers of school reform. The goals of reform and the methods employed are obviously important. But unless the reformers have a combination of personal, experiential, and stylistic characteristics, the outcome is at best problematic and at worst a basis for predicting failure. I have not been, as I could not be, commendably clear about that combination. What I am certain of is that our failure to be clear about this issue can no longer be ignored. I am also certain that when we begin to study the reformers — studies beset with thorny conceptual and methodological potholes — we will learn a great deal from people like the authors of this book.

Seymour B. Sarason
Yale University

P.S. Anticipating the reactions of the authors to this introduction, I told them they were not obliged to use it even though they had requested it. I also intimated that if they did not use it, our friendship would be adversely affected. An agreement is an agreement, I said, and keeping agreements goes a long way to explain why you are still at Louis Armstrong Middle School after so many years.

Acknowledgments

We want to thank the many people to whom we are obliged for the help and support they offered. We are thankful to the parents and staff of the Louis Armstrong Middle School for the patience, warmth, and acceptance they have consistently extended to us. We are also grateful to our many colleagues at the college, some of whom worked directly with us, others of whom offered advice and encouragement.

We are particularly indebted to the leadership of the college, particularly Saul Cohen and the late John Lidstone, who were instrumental in creating the collaboration that forms the basis of this book. Throughout the collaboration we have benefited from the wisdom of Seymour Sarason. His sharp insights and his willingness to listen have been invaluable. We also want to acknowledge the contribution of Sharon Salerno, whose dedication and skill in translating our indecipherable scribbling into readable text was an inestimable aid. Finally, we thank our wives, Naomi Trubowitz and Virginia Longo, for the patience they exhibited and the encouragement they offered, not only during the time this book was written, but through the many years we have been engaged in the collaboration.

PART I

THE COLLABORATION
Beginning and Background

Introduction

We began our effort to collaborate with the Louis Armstrong Middle School (LAMS) with one primary purpose in mind: We wanted to be part of an effort to improve the ways in which the education of our early adolescent population was conducted. That was the initial impetus for our endeavor and the major goal which guided our efforts. From the beginning, however, it was clear that a second goal, that of working successfully with the school, must be given equal attention. Collaboration was not then — nor is it now — our solitary purpose. It represents primarily a means by which interested parties can better serve the needs of educating our youth. How successfully the collaborative effort is conducted, however, will eventually dictate the quality of any other contribution an external agency can make to the functioning of schools. Thus, the quality of the collaboration effort often assumes primary importance for those conducting it, though this is usually secondary in intent. The process of the collaboration simply cannot be separated from the goal of implementing content.

While we began with the view that the collaborative process was a means and not an end, we were not without some definite ideas about what the process could contribute and what we needed to do to succeed. These were based on our prior experience with the schools. Such ideas, some clearly understood and others applied almost intuitively, have served us well over the years. Surely they were not as clear to us at the beginning as they are now, but as our understanding deepened over time, we tried to bring to a conscious level of understanding the major operating principles which have guided our behavior.

What follows is a list of those principles. We offer them because they provide a foundation for what is shared in this book. These ideas have informed much of what we attempted to do and served as guides to our behavior. The reader will note their recurrence throughout the book. You will also note that we violate them from time to time, for we have tried to use them as guides rather than as molds for program operation. They are intended to be instructive rather than prescriptive. Our hope is that they may serve as directional indicators in an enterprise that has all too few of them.

HOW WE STARTED

1. We tried to gain the support of top leadership at the two institutions.

The further up the line of the hierarchy of both institutions this support goes, the better. Interinstitutional arrangements between large bureaucratic organizations are complicated and difficult, if not impossible, to manage at lower levels without adequate support from the top. The sheer weight of bureaucratic regulations can thwart the initiation of these efforts if such help is not forthcoming.

Beyond the necessity of firm commitment and support at the top, what is critically important to the success of a collaborative enterprise is the quality of the school's leadership at the immediate level. Both institutions must be represented by individuals who are not only competent but also actively interested in exploiting the potential of such a joint venture. Our experience has been that this is more problematic for the schools than for the college. It would be extremely rare for members of the college staff to be given such a responsibility without their consent. Almost without exception, it would be a chosen rather than assigned task. Schools, on the other hand, can be "selected" for such involvement by superiors who are convinced that they will benefit. Further, changes in school leadership are not infrequent. Projects that begin with strong, supportive school leaders can later find themselves engaged in a collaboration with a less enthusiastic partner, or one with a limited vision of what can be accomplished together. Avoiding such long-term erosion is part of the challenge, but it is imperative that such efforts begin with committed, competent leadership.

2. We recognized that school-college relations have a problematic history.

The pursuit of responsibilities peculiar to their unique roles has led the schools and the colleges to a different emphasis regarding their view of the educational process. The schools focus on the programmatic, on how to deliver educational services to their students in the most efficient and effective manner. The colleges, in their training of teachers, have been more concerned with the theoretical underpinnings of that education process and what research has to contribute to an understanding of it. At their best, these roles can be complementary, but in actual practice they are often in conflict.

The source of the difficulty is not hard to understand. The genius of school organization is the ability of practitioners to routinize process. This is both the greatest strength and the greatest weakness of schools. Once routines have been established, a great deal of energy is conserved that would otherwise be wasted in making day-to-day decisions about what to do and how to do it. That energy can then be applied to other useful educational purposes. Over time, however, the very routines that once liberated energy can have a deadening effect. Because this happens slowly over a long period, those involved can experience a loss of enthusiasm and spontaneity without being fully aware of either the source of the problem or its full impact, which is even worse.

The colleges, to their credit, frequently challenge the continuing efficacy of many of these routines. That they do not always do this wisely or well is the source of a great deal of friction and misunderstanding. Because those from the college enjoy the luxury of advocating solutions from a distance, they often give less thought than is necessary to some of the practical consequences of their theories. This has fueled a continuing tension between colleges and schools. The former are often looked to for ideas, but are also resented for their implied or direct criticism of current practice.

Anyone who would attempt to create a collaborative venture between these two institutions should be aware of this troubled history, as well as the many failed efforts at jointly sponsoring innovation or change. Both our prior planning and subsequent behavior were informed by a continual review of these differences in emphasis. We worked hard to maintain an awareness that the consequences for decision-making in the schools fall unevenly upon the collaborative partners. We made it a working principle to defer to the judgment of school leadership on issues they were either unable to support or believed would present them with major problems.

3. We tried to combine flexibility of operation with clarity of vision.

It is extremely helpful to have a long-term vision of what one intends to accomplish through the collaborative process. This should not be mistaken to mean that you start with a full set of beliefs. There is a need to leave room to grow and learn, to change direction when circumstances warrant or require it, and to respond to one's intuitive sense of what the environment may demand. Usually one begins with a broad vision and a staff that values and respects people. If our experience can serve as a guide, much redirection will be required during the lifetime of most projects. Overplanning and excess in setting goals can lead to the type of operational inflexibility that will frustrate the best intentions; remember that all of us find it easier to talk about change than to engage in it. Even in collaborative projects intended to bring about change, there will be much unconscious resistance. Sarason (1995) says it well:

> In addition to death and taxes you can count on individuals and the settings in which they work to resist change very soon after they have requested help to change. That is true not only for "them" but for you and me. Change consists of unlearning and learning but far too many so-called change agents gloss over or totally ignore the turmoil that unlearning unleashes. Verbalizing the desire to change is easy; taking actions to change reveals how much we treasure our symptoms. That is as true for us as individuals as it is for a collectivity like a school. (p. 3)

In brief, one does not necessarily begin with a rock-ribbed set of beliefs and specific goals. Much of what one does is intuitive and experimental at the beginning and becomes more explicit only with time. None of this is intended to denigrate the need for vision or planning. No project can succeed without a strong sense of purpose and direction. We note the need for flexibility because experience has taught us that there will be frequent shifts of direction due to changes in personnel, altered circumstances, and unanticipated opportunities. It is useful to view the collaboration process as guided by a general plan of action rather than a plan requiring that certain ideas be implemented. We will note throughout the tendency of planners to have greater regard for their design than their circumstances.

4. We operated on the principle that the collaboration had to be of mutual benefit to the partners involved.

It was clear to us from the beginning that the collaboration would be short-lived if both parties involved did not find that at least some of their central needs were served. We tried to operate on the basis of enlightened self-interest, and thus ensure that both institutions understood the ways that the collaboration could meet specified goals that were of interest to them. What we tried to avoid was a lop-sided view of the cooperative process in which one institution was providing resources to "help" the other without a clear sense of the benefits it was receiving.

We found there was considerable misunderstanding in this regard on both parts, but for different reasons. Sometimes college staff assumed they were helping (conducting "research" for example), when those in the schools felt they were receiving nothing or simply being exploited. In other instances, college personnel saw themselves as providing services that would help improve school operation, a noble intention but one that usually had little staying power. Conversely, those in the schools too often felt that merely providing a site for college staff or trainees to work in represented a satisfactory trade-off that provided equitable benefits. From the college standpoint, housing such activity in the schools was beneficial only if considerable cooperation regarding the particular activities were forthcoming. Simply "housing" the personnel or programs was insufficient for their success.

The truth or fairness of these responses are not the issue. What one must understand is that perception matters: What is perceived as real is real in its consequences. For a collaboration to prosper over an extended period requires that participants believe that important and useful purposes are being accomplished. To the extent that this is not the case, the duration of the partnership is at risk.

5. We accepted the fact that conflict and resistance to change are constants in the bureaucratic environment.

Most collaborative efforts appear to be predicated on the assumption that the changes or vision of the intended partnership will be accepted rather than resisted by the larger educational community. That is not often the case, and those who hold such a view are likely to experience a cruel comeuppance. It would be wise to begin with the recognition that managing conflict and dealing with resistance to change are necessary components of the process. One should be prepared for—rather than shocked by—their likely occurrence. This is one of the predictable problems that we treat at some length in a later chapter.

A major difficulty is that even the concept of predictable problems is misunderstood by many who become involved in collaborative projects. One discusses them because of the high probability of their occurrence, and not to promote the illusion that they can be avoided. Too often, however, those involved in such ventures assume that "known" problems can be avoided. Proponents acknowledge their existence but frequently assume that such awareness will allow them to circumvent the truly difficult parts. In the majority of cases that is not possible and, beyond that, it is often unwise. Not all conflict can or should be avoided. If one were to ask most people what comes to mind when they hear the word *conflict*, the images or terms that surface will invariably be negative. Yet if we think about it long enough, most of us understand that conflict has many positive attributes as well. Conflict can deepen understanding, force a reexamination of views, and provide greater clarity about what we believe and why we value these beliefs. It can also make us look at potential outcomes, examine the practicality of proposals, and consider in advance the likely obstacles that may be encountered.

In any event, our experience is that identifying likely problems does not always improve your ability to escape them. The goal needs to be how to manage, and not totally avoid, conflict. This is particularly true of the change process. Few of us face change in our essential routines without encountering some degree of tension and stress. That this often leads to resistance and even conflict should not surprise us. The good news is that the full dimensions of the process, if accepted and productively managed, can have highly rewarding results.

6. We recognized that while beginnings are extremely important, maintenance is the more difficult challenge.

Those involved in projects such as these are intensely aware of the importance of getting off to a good start. Much energy and effort go into initiating activities, since it is understood they will have a lingering impact on how the project is viewed. Such an investment of time is both wise and necessary. It is vital to begin well.

Conversely, maintaining what has been successfully implemented is a concept not accorded the respect it deserves, and usually is given too little attention. As we noted earlier, most large schools focus heavily on developing routines that provide regularized procedure for dealing with the major issues facing the professional staff. In the beginning, collaborative efforts are primarily aimed at making adjustments to or changes in these procedures. When this has been accomplished, however, a program of maintenance must be instituted, or hard won gains are at risk of being lost to the tendency of institutions to return to a previously established equilibrium. Thus, maintenance becomes a difficult but necessary long-term responsibility. What makes this even more challenging is that ensuring the continuance of new approaches must often be conducted at the same time that other changes are making considerable demands on staff energy and resources.

Maintenance of change represents a formidable challenge. Large urban school systems tend to develop a provincialism of their own. Because these systems are big and have their own history, the professional staff has access to a considerable amount of internal experience. They have learned to draw heavily upon this background. However, being big does not always mean the best procedures have been chosen; indeed, size can severely limit variety. Large bureaucracies tend to homogenize rather than encourage differences. The general tendency of such bureaucracies to control, to routinize processes, causes them to be distrustful and even disdainful of differences in procedure or approach. It is the nature of such large systems that they generate constant pressure to return to previously established norms, since the whole system is based upon implicit sets of relationships and understandings that support them. Maintaining innovative gains in such an environment requires as much — if not more — imagination and skill than was required to attain them.

7. We recognized and cultivated specific constituencies, trying to find ways to collaborate successfully.

We began with the view that there is great educational value in drawing upon the skills of diverse constituencies; our experience has only confirmed that perspective. We have consciously cultivated relationships with parents, members of the community, teachers, administrators, and students. In pursuing this goal, we sought out people who really wanted to work with us. We tried to respect differences of style and the right of staff to exercise the choice not to be involved. We offered support for those who wanted to use the opportunity to pursue topics of mutual interest and worked to remain on good terms with everyone else. Over time, we found that successful efforts encouraged others to pursue their interests, and so we were able to expand our contacts with staff. We have found that patience and staying power are absolute prerequisites in this process.

A major part of our endeavor centered around joint efforts with the teaching staff. We recognized early that our presence could provide teachers with another source of encouragement for their efforts to grow and take risks. It took us longer to recognize the great value we could provide by offering them opportunities to break out of the dullness of day-to-day school routines. We could and did provide the support teachers needed to try new things, employ different approaches, and join their talents with those of others. As we just noted, not all responded to these invitations, but those who did often found it gave them either fresh perspectives or outlets for untapped energies and skills. Schools need to provide such opportunities for their teaching staff. The classroom can be a place of professional isolation that eventually dulls teaching sensibilities. By offering the chance to break out of normal routines, we established outlets for renewal and revitalization that the system too rarely offers its teachers.

We also believed that the involvement of parents created the potential for support, encouragement, and knowledge that could enrich school life. Through such activities as periodic retreats, school-based management sessions, and parent executive board meetings, we developed the habit of shared thinking. Our stance has been to communicate respect for the suggestions, ideas, and knowledge that parents have to offer.

8. We accepted the natural ambiguity built into the college role and tried to use it as a strength rather than a weakness.

The college staff members do not have assigned roles within the school bureaucracy. Rather than trying to compensate for that lack, we sought to capitalize on its possibilities. We avoided tight role definitions and sought to maintain maximum flexibility regarding the way staff could decide to employ or exercise their skills. Such a course is not uniformly advantageous. It is a compromise which trades specificity for breadth of opportunity. One needs to determine what is lost and what is gained.

It is our view that ambiguity provided greater dividends — it maximized our freedom without imposing unacceptable costs. We believe college staff can only achieve real authority in the schools through the expertise and ability they have to offer, not by defined roles. We took the view that our position is one in which respect must be earned: It cannot be conferred by others and it has not, of course, been built into the structure of the organization. This approach is demanding, but we believe it is the only one that works from the standpoint of the college. We sought a view of the world where we worked through a prism of respect, rather than one of power.

Our experience has shown that neither responsibility nor authority is a 50–50 proposition in a college–school partnership. Such a view of collaboration would be too simplistic. As we noted previously, consequences for decisions made fall unevenly upon school staff, and so we often found ourselves in the position of deferring to the school administration on what were sensitive issues. If the power to influence is to be maintained, one must exercise the ability to retreat, to have an agenda that is not too large or nonnegotiable, and to avoid trying to accomplish too much, too fast. Our view is that we are and will remain a project in process, but we try to avoid the error of thinking that progress can or should be continuous. There will be setbacks and retreats as well as movement forward. A major task is to set up a foundation that is solid enough to sustain setbacks.

9. We learned that having the right mix of people is necessary for the success of a collaboration.

It is useful, and perhaps essential, that those who lead the college collaboration are intimately knowledgeable about the public school as an entity. There are two reasons for this: one perceived and one real. The former is that the collaborators are more likely to be welcomed if they are seen as having an intimate knowledge of the ins and outs of the system. This affords one opportunities not otherwise enjoyed. The latter reason is that such understanding greatly reduces the likelihood of errors being made out of simple naiveté or inexperience. It is not that one cannot make valuable contributions without a detailed knowledge of the school as an organization. It is just that no one wants a novice in surgery, and to take on important issues, knowledge and experience matter a great deal.

Beyond the issue of leadership, it is also important that other staff brought in by the college have the skills needed to work with personnel in the schools. This goes beyond subject matter skills. It includes respect for the people you work with, avoiding the temptation to play the role of expert, and a deep understanding that teaching is a hard, difficult endeavor for which there are no formulaic prescriptions. We were extremely careful about who we invited to work with us in the schools. We cultivated the view that all bureaucracies, including our own, suffered from an organizational form of arteriosclerosis. An important part of our role is to get practitioners to step back and look at the whole picture. This included trying to provide time and opportunity to reflect about the practices in which all of us are engaged.

Because the college staff is not grounded in the moment-by-moment reality of the schools or their need to survive daily challenges, we can focus more on vision. The college environment provides its staff with ample opportunity to talk and think together. We tried to find ways we could offer that opportunity to others. We invited school staff to talk about their work in the school. Most people welcome someone who will pay attention to what they are doing, to the quality of the effort and their reflections about it. If there is someone who can be entrusted with their inner thoughts, people will share them. We tried to be that someone for the school staff. We did this by trying to earn and keep their trust. As Sarason (1995) put it, "Fear is the enemy of trust, and trust is the interpersonal vehicle by means of which different personal worlds can begin to overlap" (p. 15). Teachers need to feel there is somebody else in the school who cares a lot about what they are doing and speaks their language.

10. We recognized that a key to what we could contribute centered around our ability to provide school personnel with an outsider's view of the way the institution was functioning.

We worked from the conscious perspective that a major contribution of the college is an outsider's view of program operation, routines, and maintenance procedures. One of the unique advantages of not having a defined role in a system is that you are not part of its organized response to issues large and small. We understood early that we could play a useful role by offering an external perspective, asking questions about what was happening, and observing events from a different vantage point. The college staff had the luxury of giving additional thought to what was being attempted and why. Because we did not have direct responsibility for day-to-day affairs, our thinking was less oriented to the short term; we were not bound by the immediate. We could afford to spend more time giving thought to potential solutions that were outside the normal patterns of response.

Given this perspective, it was essential that we not become part of the routine operation of the school. To do that would be to negate a major strength and weaken the quality of the contribution we could make. We recognized that if we could avoid being drawn into the school's traditional orbit and yet not become too theory-bound or unrealistic, we could be of greater service to those with whom we were working. College faculty have more time available, a precious resource which can be translated into reflection. Many of our staff also had broad experience with other school settings and they brought this experience to the collaboration. Additionally, our culture requires us to write, to analyze what we do and relate it to efforts being made elsewhere. This combination of time, experience, and an alternative perspective was the primary resource we offered the school.

REPORTING OUR RESULTS

No collaboration starts untouched by prior events or uninfluenced by the personalities and efforts of the individuals involved. Therefore, we begin the book by providing the reader with a description of the context out of which the collaboration emerged. In Chapter 1, we review the factors that led to the establishment of the collaboration and indicate the impact of people and of history on the conduct of the project.

In Part II, we give an overview of the collaborative process itself. Though our remarks are rooted in personal experience, the intent is to draw some conclusions based on that experience and the reports of collaborations elsewhere which might prove useful to others. Thus, in Chapter 2, we try to give a picture of some of the challenges to be faced by the participants in any interinstitutional arrangement. Inevitably, there are differences in beliefs, perspectives, the concept of time, and in how rewards are achieved, and these differences have the potential for deep conflict unless handled judiciously. Despite such formidable difficulties, this chapter goes on to show the rich results that can accrue from an interweaving of cultures and how the ongoing interaction between the two institutions has redounded to the benefit of both. From an analysis of the challenges and promises presented by the collaboration, we move to Chapter 3 to a consideration of the elements that affect the formation of collaborative ventures. We explore ideas that merit attention both before a collaboration begins and as it proceeds. For example, we examine the need for both focus and flexibility in implementing the collaboration and the importance of meeting the self-interest of participants. In Chapter 4, we seek to provide the reader with an understanding of what can be expected in the stages of development that collaborations typically pass through. We discuss what can be anticipated in the form of resistances, periods of acceptance and approval, times of regression, and opportunities for renewal of forward momentum. In Chapter 5, we describe predictable problems to be faced as people from two different institutions representing two different cultures move into collaborative activity. Chapters 4 and 5 are an attempt to help others prepare for the type of challenges they are likely to face.

From a more general look at the collaborative process, Chapter 6 focuses on the particulars of how the Queens College faculty and Louis Armstrong Middle School (LAMS) personnel worked together. In this chapter we detail the ways college personnel and college activity have become closely intertwined with the ongoing operation of the school. In Chapter 7, an overview is offered of the educational ideas that guided the effort and how we sought to have these beliefs implemented. A description is given of the programs that were initiated in an attempt to reach past the boundaries of the traditional curriculum and to connect the institution to people and locations beyond the confines of the school building. Chapter 8 reviews the initiation and development of an internship model that was created to train prospective teachers. The evolution of the model and its perceived strengths are described as is the contribution of these trainees to the overall collaboration. In the last two chapters, we present our reflections on the nature of the collaborative process and give our recommendations regarding the role of collaboration in educational change. We conclude with a discussion of questions regarding the project, for it is our view that collaboration between a university and a public school is a fluid process with ongoing challenges. Given that view, it struck us as symbolically appropriate to conclude with questions rather than definitive statements, a perspective that paralleled our actual experience in the schools. It has been our experience that solutions are never final and that most answers eventually lead to a new set of questions. Taken in the right spirit, this is both the challenge and the joy of ventures such as this one.

CHAPTER 1

The Context of the Collaboration:
Born Out of Controversy

AN HISTORICAL OVERVIEW

The Queens College–Louis Armstrong Middle School (I.S. 227) collaboration emerged from controversy. Two districts (Districts 24 and 30)
battled over who should have jurisdiction over I.S. 227, a school that had
just finished being built in 1979 and was scheduled to begin operation.
There were also differences among community groups about whether the
pupil population was to be restricted to the gifted or would admit a wide
range of students. The dispute continued for many months until patience
ran out and both districts agreed to cede control of the school to the
Central Board of Education. Concurrent with the interdistrict struggles
was an NAACP suit against the Board of Education for maintaining segregated schools in District 24. In deciding the case the judge made Louis
Armstrong Middle School part of the solution and mandated that it be an
integrated school that reflected the racial composition of the borough of
Queens at that time (55% minority, 45% nonminority). Since the preferred approach to achieving the desired population mix was volunteer
busing, the presence of the college was seen as a way to enhance the
attractiveness of the school to prospective students. I.S. 227 would not
have an assigned pupil population but would act as a magnet school for
the borough (i.e., county) of Queens.

Apart from the mandate that the school have an integrated pupil
population representative of the borough, those involved in the initial
planning made another key decision regarding the composition of the
student body. It was determined that a similar effort would be made to
maintain equity regarding the prior academic performance of incoming
students. Twenty-five percent of those chosen each year are performing
below grade level on standardized tests, fifty percent are on grade level,
and twenty-five percent are above. This decision, combined with the commitment to maintain heterogeneous classroom assignments, gives the
school a unique balance regarding both its overall student population and
organization.

14

THE ROLE OF LEADERSHIP

The Queens College–Louis Armstrong Middle School collaboration became a reality because two educational leaders, Saul Cohen, the President of Queens College, and Frank Macchiarola, the Chancellor of the New York City Board of Education, combined vision with a need to deal with reality. Saul Cohen wanted to communicate his view that an important mission of the college was to serve the city. He also sought to reinvigorate a school of education faculty whose morale had been severely battered by mass firings during the 1976 New York City budget crunch and by the low status afforded it by the previous college administration. In addition, Saul Cohen, unlike many college presidents, cared about precollegiate education, and recognized it as one of the most significant functions in our society.

Chancellor Macchiarola knew colleges, having been a professor at the CUNY Graduate Center. He also understood the bitterness that can grow between community school districts, having served as president of a community school board himself. His experience allowed him to see colleges as allies rather than as adversaries and to recognize that an impasse had occurred between Districts 24 and 30. He wanted the college to help calm a situation in which anger was the prevailing emotion and to deal with the realities of the NAACP litigation against the Central Board. But beyond the desire to take care of the immediate problems of interdistrict rivalry and a legal suit, for the first time in New York City, a college president and a board of education chancellor had come together to sponsor a project to develop exemplary middle school practices in a school that was to be integrated both racially and academically.

THE IMPACT OF HISTORY

The Queens College–Louis Armstrong Middle School collaboration arose out of a history of relationships between public schools and colleges that has often been characterized by conflict and hostility. Public school staff referred to college professors as woolly-headed theorists with no sense of reality about actual classrooms. College faculty warned of too intensive an involvement with the public schools and the rigid bureaucracy that dominated their operation. They pointed to innovative beginning teachers who are drawn into the morass of public school conservatism and whose energies are absorbed in survival rather than effective instruction.

The college's previous experience with collaboration had proved devastating and left a legacy which still exists to this day. The School University Teacher Education Center (SUTEC) was a jointly planned cooperative venture of the New York City Central Board of Education and Queens College. The SUTEC program was located in P. S. 76 in Long Island City and opened in 1966. At a meeting with Queens school administrators, some 18 years since the original school–college venture concluded, a principal referred back to this collaboration and remarked, "The college worked with our school and they didn't know what they were doing. The result was chaos." That one-sided view has continued to be put forward regardless of counter claims by the college staff who were involved. The impact of this collaboration's failure was so powerful that even without performing a careful analysis of the project, we absorbed some lessons from its demise and sought to avoid the pitfalls of this prior effort between Queens College and the Board of Education.

What we discovered in examining this effort was that it began with a faulty view of how a school should be run. In this early project the plan was for co-principals, one from the Board of Education and the other from the college. Both of us, as ex-public school administrators, realized that there could be only one head of a school. Otherwise confusion would likely reign with parents and particularly with teachers, who would be unsure of the person with whom they should confer. We saw our authority coming from our expertise — our ability to work with people, identify problems, guide decision-making, and provide resources. We knew also that a principal needed a compatible person with whom to work and we backed the principal's choice for assistant principal.

The SUTEC project was initiated by a group of "true believers" who thought that traditional education was not meeting the needs of children. They envisioned a school in which student decision-making, hands-on experiences, and open curriculum choices would pervade the day. As one participant put it after the project's demise, "We saw ourselves introducing a whole new approach to education. We wanted everything to change all at once. As I look back I realize we bit off more than we could chew."

We saw from the SUTEC experience and from our many years in other schools that trying to accomplish too much too fast leads to frustration and failure. We envisioned a new kind of middle school but we did not approach the Louis Armstrong project like saviors with the message from above. We did not attempt to institute what could not be done, for the result would have damaged our efforts to work effectively with Board of Education personnel. We recognized that good ideas will not be adopted automatically and that they are only accepted into regular practice through patience and persistence.

Another observation of what occurred during the SUTEC project indicated an inadequate view of how change occurs. Unlike our predecessors we realized that we were entering an existing culture with its own set of values and that an ongoing aim would be to achieve some consensus of view. We did not take acceptance of our ideas for granted. Rather, we saw our initial goals as limited and concrete. We sought to emphasize immediate problems rather than long-term issues. We did not enter the collaboration burdened by a need to incorporate our own vision *en toto* within a prescribed length of time. We assumed a strategy of gradualism, which recognized a continuum from what education is to what education could be and accepted the need to traverse that gap slowly.

A difficulty for the SUTEC project and one that other school–college collaborations face was finding a sufficient number of college faculty willing to spend extended periods of time at the school and who had the ability to work well with public school personnel. Some professors came to the SUTEC endeavor armed with firm views supportive of open education for which they sought speedy implementation. There was a failure to understand that the task of establishing a new educational idea calls not only for expertise but an ability to be accepted as part of the social structure of the school. Public school staffs will welcome professors as colleagues after a period of time in which they have not only shown their skill as professionals but have also demonstrated an ability to listen, to empathize, and to identify with the trials and tribulations of classroom teaching. They do not accord the same welcome to professors who come to the school as visiting experts.

We note this early collaborative experience to emphasize that the context within which we began to work was one in which most previous school–college partnerships had been characterized as failures. We have come to understand more clearly than ever that all one needs to do to "fail" is not meet what are often excessive and unrealistic expectations for success.

This background created an atmosphere of skepticism for both professors and public school personnel. The distance between the college and public school remained wide, since the university reward system discouraged service in the field as opposed to writing for publication. The task facing us as we began our collaboration was to recognize the effect of these constraints and to develop support in the struggle to modify the attitudes of both public school and college staff about the potential advantages of working together.

THE INTERPLAY OF PERSONALITIES

The Queens College–Louis Armstrong Middle School collaboration came into being because it brought together a diverse group of personalities who, although they may have had different motivations and experiences, were able to find common ground and to work together in ways that supported school–college relationships.

The first principal was a former district superintendent (Anthony San Filippo) who described himself as a bureaucrat which, in his terms, meant someone who followed orders, displayed loyalty to his superiors, and attempted to implement Board of Education curricula mandates and instructions to the best of his ability. He took pride in the system and his role in it and resented those who would disparage the efforts that the schools were making. His loyalty led him to try mightily to implement the design for the school agreed to by Queens College and the Board of Education, even though he may have disagreed with some of its elements. In addition, the fact that a few months earlier his contract as district superintendent of the adjoining district had not been renewed also had an important effect on his behavior: It made him especially sensitive to the constituencies that had any role to play in evaluating his performance as school administrator. He felt that in his former position he had given insufficient attention to gaining the support of the various groups involved in the educational process. He was determined that this time he would be effective at constituency building.

Then there was the involvement of the Dean of Teacher Education (John Lidstone) whose interest in the project was evidenced by his regular visits to the school, the frequent meetings he convened to assess project progress, and his writing of articles describing life in the collaboration. His background as public school teacher and administrator, along with his work in schools as a student teacher supervisor, made him a perceptive observer of current school problems. His special commitment to art education had much to do with the curriculum's inclusion of a strong art component.

There were also the professors who saw themselves as doers, eager to implement their views of education, whose entire history had been one of working with schools, and who found personal satisfaction from involvement in schools. The chairperson of the Department of Secondary Education (Clarence Bunch) was a former Professor of Art Education, who was another advocate of the arts for children. His role as Chairperson allowed him to make LAMS the center for art education student teachers and he assumed personal responsibility for their supervision. We were also fortunate to have the involvement of a professor (Dr. Robert Edgar) who had been at the college for over 30 years. During this time he was periodically involved in field projects. But in the twilight of his career his commitment and involvement at LAMS were exceeded by none. He worked with the social studies teachers at the school, held regular meetings, taught classes, and went on class trips. He also acted as a member of the Social Studies Department and spent at least three days a week at the school.

There were also the authors, both of whom, at different times, served as liaisons between the college and public school. We knew about public education from working as teachers and administrators in various schools, and were also very familiar with the college, serving in administrative capacities and teaching in areas such as administration, school and community relations, and methods courses in the teaching of mathematics, social studies, and language arts. Thus our experience gave us knowledge of both the public school and college.

Sometimes it is difficult to distinguish between value that is real and value that accrues from the merely symbolic. The symbolic, if it communicates strongly enough, has the same effect as the real. Our personal history was of great symbolic value. The fact that we had been teachers and administrators in the school offered the staff some confidence that we understood the problems of the schools. It reassured the Board of Education personnel, from superintendents to the school teachers and assistant principal, and removed the argument about each of us that, if put into words, might be: "Oh, he's one of those idealistic college teachers who hasn't been near a classroom in twenty years. How can he understand?"

Most important, we knew what it was like to be a principal. The differences between a college professor and a school administrator are enormous. A college professor is almost totally autonomous. A public school principal is besieged by pressures from all sides—from subordinates, parents, community groups, and teachers. Professors have little sense of time urgency. Schools with large student populations run by routine, and the clock is followed meticulously, lest buses are missed, classes move into occupied rooms, and general logistic confusion reigns. It became one of our tasks to help college people become aware of what it is to be a school administrator.

There were other professors who joined the collaboration at the beginning and became significant players in its development. They included Linda Catelli, who helped to shape a unique physical education program, and Lee Ann Truesdell, who became mentor to the special education staff.

The mixture of personalities carried over to the teaching staff, who were all New York City licensed teachers of different ages and experience. Some came to LAMS because of a desire to work in an exciting atmosphere, and others came to escape a chaotic situation. Some came because they had transfer rights based on seniority and others obtained a position because they were recommended by a college professor or had a specialty in an area of teacher shortage, such as mathematics or science. They were a diverse group representing various levels of motivation, experience, and expertise.

INITIAL PROBLEMS

The Queens College–Louis Armstrong Middle School collaboration began surrounded by problems. The mandate for student integration automatically eliminated large numbers of neighborhood children, since the immediate area was predominantly minority group. It was difficult for families living within walking distance of the school to understand why their children could not be admitted because of the necessity for integration. One result was a steady stream of politicians seeking special dispensation for families of their constituents. Another effect is that a level of residual bitterness remains. The school resides in a community that it does not fully serve, an issue we have taken steps to try and address. For example, over the years the school has conducted foreign language classes for adults during the day, adult education classes four nights a week, and after-school tutorial and Saturday morning classes for students from the local community.

Another problem came as other Queens districts saw a threat in the emergence of a school that would draw students from throughout the borough. They looked with anger and concern at the possibility that this "special" school would take away their best pupils. Staff in these schools reacted in various ways. Some "forgot" to distribute the recruitment material describing LAMS. Others both actively discouraged parents from transferring children to the new school and encouraged the families of pupils with a history of trouble to take advantage of this new opportunity. Still others set up special programs to provide an attractive alternative for students who might otherwise have transferred to LAMS.

Competition for students led to expressions of envy. It was common to hear remarks such as "They do well because they have all that extra money" or "Of course, the students achieve. Look at all the extra resources the college provides." Other forms of early antagonism showed in the attitudes of some parents. Different parent groups sought immediate attention for the children they represented. Special education parents wanted a quick time table for the admission of their students. Another group demanded that classes for the gifted be established. They were seeking what they had in their neighborhood elementary schools. Both groups expressed their displeasure at the collaboration when there was no ready response to their demands. Despite the pressure, there was no deviation from the plan to build student population slowly and to maintain heterogeneous grouping.

Initial meetings with Queens College faculty revealed animosity on the part of some professors. Previous unsatisfactory experience with public schools had influenced their reaction to any effort at collaboration. One professor proclaimed, "By having the opportunity to choose staff you're creating an unrealistic situation. The school staff should include mediocre teachers as well as good ones. If we're going to learn from the school, you need more reality."

Another professor protested that the school contained insufficient numbers of African-American children, even though the majority–minority breakdown reflected the racial composition of the borough. She advised that the only way to get change is to confront people and introduce conflict. It did not strike us as a way most conducive to establishing good relationships.

Most of the faculty chose to observe the project from afar, with a small vocal group advocating that the college remain removed from any contact with the board of education. The response of faculty from other college departments was apathy. Those academicians outside the School of Education saw little reason for becoming involved in the world of schools.

Despite any of the problems mentioned, the collaboration began with enthusiasm, hope, commitment, and pride of ownership. There was the support of the college president and the chancellor which brought both psychological encouragement and access to resources. There was the involvement of key personnel in the school of Education (Dean of Teacher Education, Associate Dean of Education, Chairperson of the Department of Secondary Education) which contributed sources of power to the project. There was the small cadre of professors who volunteered hundreds of hours to read the resumes of teacher applicants and to attend weekly evening meetings with parents and community representatives to prepare for the opening of school. There was the high visibility of college staff with the Director and professors present daily at the school. (A Queens College office was set up at the school to provide a working area for faculty.) There was the ongoing interaction of parents, teachers, administrators, and professors at social occasions, at meetings, and at school functions such as plays and musical presentation.

We began with a vision of what a middle school could be. It was stated in our first book (Trubowitz, Duncan, Fibkins, Longo, & Sarason, 1984):

> We had dreams of making integration work successfully in an urban school, of creating a place where children of different races, languages, and backgrounds would be a source of richness rather than divisiveness. We had dreams of undoing the stereotype of 10 to 14 year-olds as rebellious creatures who persist in being uninvolved with learning and are alienated from adults, and of developing a middle school that looked at children as the soul of an enterprise rather than as

its enemy. We envisioned a school where maintenance of order would not be the end, where unnecessary rules would be avoided, and where children experienced unconditional positive response. We wanted a school where each child would be known well by at least one adult. We saw a school that rejected segregation of students whether on the basis of race, ability, or handicap. We pictured a school in which teachers would be willing to take risks. We hoped for a situation in which college personnel would be accepted by public school staff as partners in the effort to improve education. We sought the development of cooperative relationships among school, college, and community in which everyone could identify with common purposes. We saw a school that would develop curriculum rather than be restricted by it. We dreamed of a school constantly involved in the process of improving itself. We wanted a school that recognized the arts as integral to education. We envisioned a learning environment that would accommodate the learning styles and interests of each child. We wanted a school that saw community education as not only a way of providing learning opportunities for community residents, but also as a way of utilizing the many experiences and skills of neighborhood people. We dreamed of a school that was out of the ordinary, that could combine all that was best for children. (pp. 65–66)

We soon realized that visions are not simply implemented. We saw that clarifying roles and establishing personal and professional credentials takes time. We posed questions that we face to this day.

- How can we continue to implement change to bring the school closer to the ideas expressed in the original design?
- How can we create and maintain a situation in which teachers and administrators will be more willing to accept and utilize Queens College resources?
- How can we help a school and its staff to take the risk of moving beyond what they are accustomed to doing?
- How can we use the experience of working with the Louis Armstrong Middle School to affect teacher education at the college?
- How can we maintain what is effective, modify what needs to be improved, and keep our vision alive?

From the outset, changes were incorporated into the school's operation. A longer school day was established, allowing students to get as much art and music as they did the traditional academic subjects. The teacher education program was vitalized by the fact that some college classes were conducted at the school, providing prospective teachers with ready access to middle school students. In our attempt to personalize instruction, a mentorship program was established with teachers, parents, and community residents serving as guides to individual students. The school initiated an Early Bird program in which teaching staff identified an activity based on their interest and students opted to participate; the groups met prior to the school's official opening and represented a matching of teacher and student interest. Saturday classes at the college were organized, and provided a place for curriculum experimentation to occur. An internship program in which graduate students in education served at the school three days a week added to the number of adults interacting with students. At the end of the first year, a school–community museum was established and became a place to display the work of children and local adults. The college's Marriage and Family Counseling program created a field site at Louis Armstrong and worked directly with the families of students who were experiencing problems.

These programmatic, organizational, and scheduling changes lent an initial vitality to the project. But a school–college collaboration is a living organism subject to environmental pressures, and for it to remain viable and to develop demanded ongoing adaptation to changing circumstances. The result has been that some initial activities remain as part of the project to this day while others have been expanded and have become institutionalized. Still others have disappeared, smothered by the course of events. For example, the Early Bird program is now an integral part of school operation. Saturday classes at the college continue. The use of the school as a site for college courses has grown. The museum regularly exhibits the results of class activity and the work of local artists. The mentorship program has grown into advisories in which groups of youngsters meet regularly with an adult to discuss topics of shared interest. On the other hand, with changing leadership the emphasis on the arts has been lost and we have had to modify the Queens College Marriage and Family Counseling program to make use of volunteer graduates and student interns from another university.

We have found that the road to program development is filled with obstacles, and steady progress is by no means guaranteed. In later chapters we will discuss in greater detail the activities which have been started and continue and those which have been started and no longer exist.

The central fact remains that the Queens College–Louis Armstrong Middle School collaboration, born out of controversy, supported by visionary leadership, impacted by history, and affected by diverse personalities, is now concluding its seventeenth year of operation and continues in its effort to implement exemplary middle school education.

PART II

THE COLLABORATION
How It Works

CHAPTER 2

Collaboration: Challenge and Promise

Collaboration has become one of the positive buzz words in education. Within the 1990s, numerous collaborative efforts have been mounted in a manner that has become common to attempts at innovation, with the result that excessive expectations have been stimulated regarding the contributions that they can make. As with many prior efforts at improvement or reform, there is a rich potential in the overall concept that should not be obscured by the extraordinary hype that too often accompanies attempts to make educational change. Innovative efforts in America's schools have been hampered by a predictable—if destructive—pattern since the 1960s. In an inversion of Shakespeare's line, too many have ended up damned by great praise. If one were to judge by past history, the unrealistic set of expectations that quickly attach themselves to any new approach will eventually lead to widespread abandonment before its more limited—but actual—promise can be realized. Too often in all this, early proponents of new ideas have been guilty of promoting the kind of heightened expectations that are eventually used to declare the effort a failure.

A VIEW OF COLLABORATION

Let us begin then by stating our view of what collaboration is not. It does not represent a panacea for the major ills of education. Nor does it provide a commonly agreed upon set of principles that can be systematically applied in ways that allow outcomes to be measured against prior performance. Indeed, there is not even uniform agreement about precisely what constitutes a true collaboration as opposed to a partnership or a jointly sponsored venture. Mainly, what seems to define a collaborative effort is the attempt to bring in support and know-how from sources outside of the normal boundaries of the school as an institution. Part of the attraction of collaborative arrangements is the additional resources they can bring to bear upon the mounting set of problems educators face.

27

A central feature of collaboration, one that is often more implicit than explicit, is the capacity to provide an outside view of the day-to-day workings of the organization. This potential for providing fresh perspective can be a key attraction for those seeking new ways to deal with seemingly intractable problems. It can also be the source of considerable friction. Interinstitutional arrangements are fraught with peril for both groups since the mission, basic operational procedures, and reward systems often differ greatly. Additionally, individuals who are not part of the public school organization and do not have a defined role within it are frequently viewed with a combination of skepticism and distrust.

Perhaps a classic example of the way external groups are viewed is illustrated in a piece of humor we have heard repeated on several occasions. To the question, "What are three of the biggest lies ever told?", the answer put forward is: "The check is in the mail, I will marry you when my divorce becomes final, and I am from the college and I am here to help you." Like many such jokes, the story can be retold with other agencies (like the state education department) or individuals (like superintendents) used as the foil. What is a constant is the suspicion on the part of school recipients that nothing good will be provided by those outside of their own immediate circle. It reflects a disposition to believe that irrespective of what is promised or intended, what will probably result is more work and greater strain for those receiving the "gift." Such views are not without a basis in reality. They do reflect the experience of some and must be viewed as part of the real world with which any collaboration must contend.

PUBLIC SCHOOL AND COLLEGE: DIFFERENT APPROACHES TO COLLABORATION

All this is to say that collaboration is not an easy or a smooth process. It requires skill on the part of primary participants and must be worked at with a combination of tenacity and persistence. Nothing is automatic and breakdowns in trust, procedures, or processes are a constant threat. Four major issues that we found ourselves contending with were the following: differences in educational perspective between college and school staff, differences in what efforts are respected and rewarded by the two institutions, a divergent sense of time regarding the work day and/or week, and the lack of a previously defined role for college staff within the school organization. Each of these issues present their own set of difficulties.

A major problem was that of differences in educational beliefs or perspective. These differences generally center around the theoretical underpinnings of the teaching/learning process; they will tend to surface once collaborative teams have moved past preliminary discussions and begin to focus on actual implementation. What seems like a shared vision built on common agreements can founder when attempts are made to translate it into particular student and teacher behaviors.

Seymour Sarason has spoken often of putting ideas into currency before they are put into action. That is a sound principle. There needs to be detailed, in-depth discussions of goals, expectations, and behaviors if a cooperative effort is to be successful. Most importantly, there must be a commitment to working out unforseen differences and difficulties that will arise as ideas are translated into specific practices that have clear implications for particular individuals. The basic fact that actions have consequences leads to one of the major dilemmas faced by those involved in joint school collaborative college efforts. Consequences in a collaborative simply do not affect all parties equally. Those with defined roles and assigned responsibilities within the institution will bear the brunt of any blame for mistakes in judgment that lead to serious problems. Since the collaboration essentially takes place in the school, there is an accountability assigned by law and parental expectations to the role of teacher or administrator that is far greater than that of any college faculty. The fact is that in the event of failure, college personnel can simply leave, perhaps with their reputation somewhat tarnished, but not faced with continually working in a problematic environment.

These uneven consequences have implications for planning, decision-making, and participation. College staff need to exercise care so that their virtual immunity from the direct consequences of their actions will not cause them to be unresponsive to the legitimate concerns of school staff or cavalier in their consideration of the full range of possible outcomes. There must be a reasonable deference to those whose lives will be most directly affected by decisions. This should be balanced, however, with a continuing commitment to the vision that informed the collaboration. The existence of a possible downside for any effort made should not be allowed to paralyze attempts to make needed changes. One of the primary weaknesses of collaboration may be the tendency of outsiders to defer to the expertise of those most familiar with the conventions of the school as an institution. A number of the recent studies of education that were highly touted — e.g., *A Nation at Risk* (National Commission on Excellence in Education, 1986) — put forward some surprisingly mundane solutions. Perhaps these were viewed as a wise accommodation between the business people and educators who formed the task forces that produced the reports, but it appeared to compromise the more serious intent of making improvements. That is the danger of deferring to the pressures of accom-

modating the partnership rather than maintaining focus on the goals of
the collaboration. Thus, the ongoing challenge is how to keep the vision
in view without pressuring schools to implement ideas for which they are
totally unprepared.

TOLERATING AMBIGUITY

None of this is easy. It is all a question of maintaining balance and
proportion in circumstances where there are often no sure guides. Those
responsible for furthering the purposes of the collaboration need to be
aware that tolerating a high degree of ambiguity while continuing to
remain focused on key goals is part of the required process. Because
college staff will be operating in an atmosphere where the consequences
for decisions fall unequally, it is vital that they give a great deal of thought
to the proposals they put forward. An unwise deference is a weakness, and
so is the presumption that any change will be an improvement. There is a
shop-worn characterization of school–college attitudes toward innovation
that is part caricature and part truth: Schools pursue progress while attempting to avoid any real change, while the colleges pursue change without attempting to determine whether it leads to any real progress. As with
many such epigrams, this one contains enough truth regarding essential
tendencies within both institutions that it is good to keep it in mind.

DIFFERENCES IN THE CONCEPT OF TIME

One also needs to take note of the difficulty presented by differences in the
concept of time and the reward systems of the two institutions. Because of
the nature of their work schedules, college faculty generally have far more
free time than school staff. That can be both a bone of contention and a
source of real strength. The contention can arise over the different sense
of time that the two institutions inculcate in those working within them.
The college faculty are used to flexible schedules that do not require
them to be at work daily nor to observe set hours apart from their direct
responsibilities. There is far more discretionary time that can be used for
research, reflection, and preparation. The luxury of time that such schedules provide can be a real plus to whatever activity they are working on.
     Classroom teachers, on the other hand, have a much more fixed
schedule and a reasonably full teaching day. Unlike college staff, who will
generally have other responsibilities and whose work schedule will only
call for them to appear sporadically at the school, teachers must put in a

full day five days a week. There is fertile ground here for both resentment and misunderstanding regarding effort, availability, and commitment, if one uses time as the major variable by which input is measured. Beyond that, conflicts in the schedules of teachers from the two institutions may frequently make it difficult to get them together. Because classroom teachers put in such a full week, it is often difficult to get them to stay after school hours to work with college staff, though this is usually the only way a reasonable block of time can be set aside for mutual effort.

It takes work and a degree of good will to insure that these different perspectives about time and the structure of the work day do not impede the ability of staff from the two institutions to work in a cooperative, mutually beneficial manner. Understanding needs to be extended by both and imaginative means must be employed to find ways to work together successfully within the confines of conflicting schedules.

The response of this particular collaboration to the problem of time was to assign several college staff to more extended roles in the school. The director of the project worked a regular five-day week, the college liaison four days a week, and the intern supervisor three. This allowed for far greater program continuity. The remaining five or six college staff assigned to the school each year spent one day a week working with staff and students on a variety of projects that were coordinated by the Director of the program. Finding college staff who are prepared to work these schedules is not always easy, since it conflicts with the norms of the college culture and takes time away from research and publications.

DIFFERENCES IN REWARD SYSTEMS

This leads directly to the next set of difficulties that we encountered. There are acute differences in the reward system or incentives employed by the two institutions. Both tenure and promotion at the college are essentially based on a record of research and publication. The pressures on college staff are both different and quite urgent regarding how one chooses to invest effort. Those in professional roles must balance and justify in their own minds the amount of time they give to preparations for teaching (as opposed to writing), whether it is the actual planning of lessons or attempts to stay involved in schools, so they can maintain an understanding of the current work environment. These are difficult choices, and it is understandable that some opt to stay away, conducting their research activities from a distance or through intermediaries in an attempt to make better use of their time. As with many such choices of efficiency over experience, much is lost. Some part of this absence of actual experience is what gives birth to the charge by those in the schools that college staff live in an ivory tower that values theory over practice. It is not a baseless charge, since the tendency is clearly rooted in the culture of the college. More time is given to reflections about the teaching and learning process than to obtaining direct hands-on experience.

However, it can also become a stereotype that clouds understanding and blocks the real contribution that college staff can make to the schools. Furthermore, this viewpoint can be used to obscure similar tendencies within the schools. Classroom teachers frequently echo this same valuing of efficiency over experience in the persistent determination to employ lecture over more student-centered learning approaches as the dominant mode of instruction. This choice of verbalizing ideas rather than having students experience them certainly allows a lot more curriculum to be "covered." But here too what we have is theory obscuring reality. What is covered is not always learned and when it is, it is often without great depth. What appears on the surface as a more efficient use of teaching time is often experienced by the learner in the form of muddled understanding. The tragedy is that neither institution offers much support for those making a serious effort to adopt other instructional styles.

We have found that the attempt to bring about change often encounters the force of a dominant teaching tradition that bridges the culture of the two institutions. The lecture format is an outgrowth of the way we organize and structure our entire educational effort. Promoting real change in such circumstances is not a simple task. In our case we have decided to make haste slowly. Change in this instance is less a decision to adopt a new instructional style then to adapt the structure in ways that invite the use of alternatives. Modifying the reward system, particularly at the college level, will be a vital part of any real effort to promote other instructional approaches. Neither the schools nor the colleges offer a rich variety of alternative models in this regard.

So it can be seen that the challenges facing school and college collaborators are many. They include keeping expectations within reasonable boundaries, dealing with initial distrust and skepticism, obtaining a balance between achieving a vision and maintaining the school as an organization, and creating a social system that allows different cultural norms of behavior to coexist.

THE POTENTIAL OF THE COLLABORATION

If what has been discussed represents some of the difficulties encountered, what then are some of the strengths a collaborative effort brings to the schools? As noted earlier, first and foremost is providing those within the institution with an outside perspective regarding its operation. The chief strength and the primary weakness of the college staff is that they are not part of the school culture. As noted, the weakness may be manifested in naive assumptions about what can be done in the school setting and how change can be brought about. The strength is that college faculty are not tied to well-defined roles, similar time constraints, or a set of expectations imposed by parents or school traditions. The absence of such constraints, if reflected upon and wisely used, can be a liberating influence. It can be used to help classroom teachers try new things and broaden their perspective about what is possible. If college personnel prove trustworthy, school staff can use them as a sounding board for concerns or as support for things they want to try, experimental efforts for which the encouragement and help of other professionals not in a supervisory relationship is available to them. That support may take the form of providing supplies and materials, extra hands, some legwork, or simply listening and responding to ideas.

It is clear that not all college staff want to participate or have the skills to contribute to such a collaborative effort. On an individual basis, what is required of them is that they combine the demands of the two cultures and make it work both personally and professionally. The issue of developing mutually beneficial arrangements is a key to making the collaboration successful. One cannot expect staff from either institution to continue participating — over an extended period — in a partnership that does not provide some benefits to each. Not all college staff have the ability to translate what they know into ideas of practical use to the schools. Even fewer have the skill to make their contribution in the school setting work to help them meet their responsibilities at the college. Given these limitations, those involved in collaborative efforts must accept the fact that the percentage of those capable of making a significant contribution is usually small and likely to remain so.

THE POWER OF JOINT EFFORTS

One of the great strength of collaboration is that it meets the need of the college community to become invested in the improvement of precollege education. That the need is too often unrecognized does not take away from its urgency. Jay Oliva, President of New York University, says it directly: "Higher education has an enormous stake in the product of our elementary and secondary schools. There must be constant interaction between the schools and higher education if the crisis in public education is to be solved" (quoted in Byrd, 1993, p. 6). It seems increasingly clear that having our public schools and colleges working in isolation from one another does not make sense. It is meaningless talk for institutions of higher education to decry the poor quality of their entering students without offering energy and resources to ameliorate the situation. A remark by Saul Cohen when he was president of Queens College captures it well: "We at the college need to cease behaving as if the 18 year-old freshman arrives on campus delivered by a stork." Higher education is clearly indebted to elementary and secondary schools for the prior education of prospective students. When examining the crisis that our schools now face in terms of increasing need and declining resources, criticism is not a sufficient response. We need to help one another.

In a similar vein, it has also become evident that teacher education programs conducted primarily in the isolation of the college campus deprive prospective teachers of necessary contact with reality. In addition, there is a growing recognition that teacher development does not terminate upon graduation from a four-year college. It needs the ongoing effort of both college faculty and public school staff to provide the nurturance, knowledge, and security to ensure continued professional growth. The schism between preservice education and inservice staff development has resulted in a conflict between two opposing points of view that has been far more damaging than instructive. Fundamental changes in American education will not be realized unless improvements in preservice education take place in conjunction with modifications in the school environment where graduates will teach. Projects that separate and target independently the improvement of teacher education, school governance, curriculum, and staff development are insufficient to overcome the power of the status quo.

In subsequent chapters we will note some of the specific accomplishments of the collaboration: positive school–college relationships, an Early Bird program, Camp Armstrong, the Louis Armstrong Museum, a community school, maintaining an integrated school, the internship program, and other aspects of good middle school education. No public school working alone could bring into being or sustain all of these ideas. It was the school–college collaboration that allowed projects like the ones mentioned to be launched and continued. What did the college contribute that allowed these unique efforts to succeed? More particularly, what roles did the college fill that helped such ideas germinate and flower, and what were the qualities of the collaboration that made for positive growth?

CREATING THE VISION

Stories abound about how institutions overwhelmed by the exigencies of daily operation lose sight of the purposes of the organization. This collaboration, like other organizations, began with a statement of mission. Both university and public school agreed to the ideas of cooperative policy-making, a community school, a dawn-to-dusk school operation, a focus on the arts, the maintenance of an integrated student population, and the implementation of effective middle school educational concepts. But running a school is a complicated process. The pressures of crises, of organizational maintenance (such as establishing schedules, distributing supplies, supervising hallways and lunchrooms, implementing bureaucratic regulations), and of meeting with teachers, parents, and students often result in a dimming of vision. In the collaboration, college personnel, free of the demands of school operation, took on the role of school conscience. We became a Greek chorus, asking questions such as the following: How do we provide for the individual in the context of heterogeneously organized classes? How do we continue to maintain an integrated school population? What are we doing to keep an emphasis on the arts? How can we make parent participation more widespread and more meaningful? How do we create a school organization that reduces student anonymity?

Our constant visibility and availability presented an embodiment of the idea that the school was to be special, to represent the essence of good middle school education. The beginning-of-the-year school–community retreat held at the college established the year's goals in line with the school's mission. The inclusion of Dr. Trubowitz, the Director of the Queens College Center for the Improvement of Education (CIE), as part of the school's administrative cabinet ensured a voice that looked beyond the need to quell the latest disturbance. It allowed an outside voice to be on the inside of school operation, permitting an external perspective on what was happening. An ongoing task of the collaboration has been to return periodically to the original vision and to note what the school was doing to revise and/or achieve its goals.

PROVIDING SUPPORT

Offering support to those working within the schools is another key task of the college staff. That role extends to the leadership of the school. Taking on the role of school principal is, as one former occupant put it, to don the mantle of Elijah. The sense of responsibility is enormous and, in many ways, it is the loneliest job in the school. Teachers have other teachers in whom to confide; but the school principal is looked to as the repository of all knowledge and is expected to be self-sufficient, the person who supports others with no need for self-support. Nothing could be farther from the truth. College personnel provide the principal with colleagues, people whom he or she could vent frustration to, discuss educational concepts, and move beyond the immediate problems to consider future possibilities. As noted earlier, to increase contact between the principal and college faculty, the design of the collaboration called for the principal to teach a course at the college. This provided hours of informal conversation before the start of class and helped to increase the sense of colleagueship between professors and principal.

An additional strategy for providing the principal with support was the establishment of an administrators' network made up of five school principals, four of whom were new to their roles. Once a month the associate dean of education and the director of the collaboration meet with the group to discuss issues of mutual interest. As with any self-help group, we have found that there is great power in knowing that you are not alone in the difficulties you are experiencing.

The value of offering school personnel the opportunity to hear and have their views heard has far-reaching importance. College staff served as listening posts within the school, providing an outlet for teachers dealing with a difficult age group. Teaching 10- to 14-year-olds immerses one in a situation where students are experiencing many emotions, some of which are expressed, some of which are clear, but many of which are not easily understood. The director of the collaboration made it a practice to wander through the school to listen to teachers as they expressed concern, asked questions, and sought recognition for what they were doing. Other professors too gave teachers with whom they worked the opportunity to express views and emotions. Listening serves as a form of caring, which teachers, encased within the four walls of their classroom, experience all too infrequently.

INTRODUCING NEW IDEAS

Schools are centers of doing. The major goal is for the organization to run smoothly. The notion of the school as a place to generate ideas is not part of its operational reality. Completing the curriculum, handling the many clerical demands, and keeping discipline are among the tasks superseding any other thoughts. The collaboration introduced an outside source of intellectual energy. Not burdened to the same degree by the day-to-day demands of maintaining the organization, we actively thought about issues confronting the school and sought ways of dealing with them.

The Early Bird program emerged out of a conversation with the Dean of the School of Education who saw it as a useful way of providing meaningful experiences for interns and student teachers. The school museum came into being when the late Dr. Bunch, Professor of Art Education, and Dr. Trubowitz were attending an art conference in Boston. As they were viewing an exhibition of paintings, Dr. Bunch almost idly remarked, "Wouldn't it be nice to have a museum in the school?" Dr. Trubowitz turned to him and replied, "Let's do it." The idea was shared with the principal, who responded with enthusiasm. The art teachers and interns also reacted positively. Dr. Bunch worked with the school staff to convert an ordinary classroom into a museum complete with exhibit cases, storage space, and track lighting. Each year the entire school and community look forward to new exhibitions, and the museum has become an expected aspect of school operation.

As college and school staff meet together in nonpressured circumstances (after school, over breakfast, at weekend retreats, at professional conferences) the school becomes a place for ideas to be generated. The value of sitting around and discussing ideas ought not to be underestimated; it is in these times of relaxed reflection that new ideas are born. The college helped to introduce thinking into a culture primarily devoted to doing. At the same time, we tried to encourage those at the college to give more thought to the practical problems that our colleagues in the school face daily. Project staff often met at the college when the school day was over to share experiences and reflect about where we were going. The sessions were invaluable in helping us clarify our thinking, deal with discouragement, and maintain a sharp focus. Surprisingly, we were criticized by several of our colleagues in the School of Education for what they saw as an unproductive use of our time — even though it was literally "our time" — spent over and above what was required.

Such misunderstanding is disturbing on at least two levels. First, the work is hard and the opportunity for reflection so critical that we felt the need to do more of it on our own time. To have that effort disparaged demonstrated a clear lack of understanding about what we were doing. Second, it was our hope that college staff might see such dialogue as something from which they could benefit. We were, after all, deeply involved in the ongoing life of the school and our experience had some obvious implications for the conduct of teacher training. We had hoped the staff would see the project as a resource. Few did. Such separation is part of life in any large organization. Collaboration provided us — as well as the school staff — more numerous opportunities to reflect about what we were doing. We continue to believe that the school and the college need more time for such reflection. The norm, unfortunately, is that in both organizations almost all the time spent is committed to maintenance of ongoing operations.

FINDING RESOURCES

There is also the problem of institutional isolation. Each school represents separate territory. Schools within blocks of each other may have little or no contact. There is little tradition of sharing resources. In the collaboration we used our knowledge and previous experience to link up with other people, groups, and organizations to find ways to enrich the school. We avoided obtaining experts for one-shot appearances, but rather worked toward the integration of resources into the ongoing functioning of the school.

The following people and accomplishments represent examples of efforts that CIE made to break down the walls of the school and obtain the help of other people and groups:

- Arthur Tobier, oral historian, came to the school to work with teachers and students to broaden their view of history to include a study of the lives of real people within the surrounding community.
- Richard Lewis, Director of the Touchstone Center and a gifted teacher, joined the school as a poet-in-residence and worked directly with students in classes to explore uses of the imagination.
- Irene Karras and John Melser, retired New York City principals, mentored the interns, supervised student teachers, and assisted new teachers.
- Joel Beller, a former high school assistant principal of science, has served as a resource for the school's science staff and has provided support for special education teachers with little prior knowledge in the subject.
- Joan Schine, Director of the Early Adolescent Helper Program, helped the school participate in the activities of that network by organizing community service and community mentorship programs.
- The collaboration applied for and received a Mott Foundation grant to set up a program of community education.
- The collaboration obtained New York Foundation of the Arts funding to support the school's art program.
- The college and the school collaborated to write a proposal that led to the U.S. Department of Education giving the school a large grant to promote activities that would help maintain an integrated school population.
- The Queens College CIE established both a principals' network and a superintendents' network to facilitate a sharing of ideas.

Thus, as a key part of its contribution to the collaboration, the college was able to extend the pool of resources available to the school. In doing so, we were able to work with school staff, as colleagues, in pushing back barriers to greater cooperation with others.

COLLEGE STAFF AS ARBITRATORS

Schools, like any organization, are made up of groups with vested interests. The college staff strove to establish itself as a disinterested member of the collaboration. This is not to say we did not express a distinct point of view, but all along we tried to listen, to show openness to other points of view, and to be respectful in our responses. Evidence that the college enjoyed a reasonable reputation for objectivity and impartiality was the fact that the Director of the Queens College Center was chosen by teachers, parents, and students to chair the school-based management team. There are a number of other examples one could cite to demonstrate this same point. The college, because of its unique role and mode of operation, has been able to play an important role as an in-school arbitrator. Again, our weakness here became a major source of strength. Because we do not have assigned roles in the school, we do not represent partisan interests and can use whatever influence we have earned to support an objective assessment of issues.

SUMMARY

In interinstitutional arrangements, cultural differences may cause conflict; but there is also the possibility that the interweaving of cultures may yield rich results. In the Queens College–Louis Armstrong Middle School collaboration, the college has helped to maintain focus on the school's mission to develop effective approaches to middle school education, to increase parent involvement, to provide professional peers for the principal, to generate a flow of ideas, to expand the pool of available resources, and to serve as arbitrator of disputes. The ongoing interaction between the two institutions continues to redound to the benefit of both. The blending of practicality and visioning and the increase in knowledge of each other has helped make Louis Armstrong a school which has achieved success, if that is to be measured by scores on achievement tests, the number of applications to the school, and the positive way the school is perceived by the larger community.

The collaboration has also bought an increased reality to the teacher education program, but the fact is that the millenium has not been reached. The road to change moves along an uncertain path, and despite almost two decades of collaboration, much remains to be done. The possibility of regression to a more traditional school organization is real and many problems remain. Part of our growth has been our ability to accept the fact that problems will indeed remain a constant. There are no final answers. We have learned to take pride in successfully meeting the challenges as they come, not in some utopian expectation that stasis can either be achieved or is desirable.

CHAPTER 3

Forging the Collaboration: Elements to Consider

Perhaps the key reflection one can offer to others considering the formation of collaborative ventures is to be prepared to tolerate high levels of ambiguity and frustration. We do not suggest that these are the means, and certainly not the ends, but they apparently are necessary concomitants to such efforts. This seems true of the change process in general, and collaboration, whatever its specific goals or conscious intent, has the issue of change as its central theme.

CHANGE: A DIFFICULT PROCESS

Making change is an endeavor fraught with much difficulty. Most of us can see the need for change in others much more clearly than we can see it in ourselves. It is a threatening prospect for individuals and for the institutions in which they work. It is always more easily spoken of than accomplished. A preliminary assessment of the Coalition of Essential Schools (Muncey & McQuillan, 1993), a national education reform movement advocating the restructuring of schools, only underscores what prior experience with change has taught us:

> (Our) findings are wide-ranging and some may appear to denigrate the coalition schools' efforts at change. This is not our intent. Our research clearly revealed that schoolwide reform will be difficult to accomplish, it will be time- and labor-intensive, and it will require rethinking and relearning on everyone's part. There are no quick fixes or miracle cures. (p. 487)

The report then goes on to list as its very first finding that in most of the schools studied, "there was not a consensus that fundamental changes in school structure or teaching practices needed to occur" (p. 487). That perspective remains a key issue and one with which those intent on developing collaborative relationships must be prepared to contend. The absence of any felt need for change must ultimately frustrate the effort to attain it. Collaboration, by its very nature, introduces new elements into the school structure. Simply to accommodate these new elements, let alone to use them purposefully, will require changes in the way the organization must function. That is why we want to emphasize that whether change is the conscious intent of the collaboration or not, those participating in it will find themselves dealing with many of the problems that are common to that process. They will occur because the simple fact of introducing outsiders into the school structure requires accommodations that in themselves necessitate a certain amount of restructuring. This is not to say that such adjustments should be mistaken for purposeful and meaningful change. To accomplish that, those involved in the collaboration must agree that certain changes are needed, that bringing them about is intended, and that there is a clear mechanism for doing so. As the report cited above makes clear, it is even possible to join a coalition whose stated purpose is restructuring and yet retain the belief that no change will be needed or required.

It appears evident then that each collaboration must work hard at developing clarity regarding its central intentions. That sounds simple. It is not. Clarity of purpose is not a given, and stating objectives in ways that lead to a common plan of action is extremely difficult. Our experience has been that it is easy to get agreements about broadly stated goals, because everyone can read their own intentions into them. The apparent consensus quickly breaks down, however, when specific plans for implementation are put forward because procedures force everyone to begin clarifying intent. It is often at this point that some very real differences will emerge. It is our view that the differences would be better identified earlier. This would lead to fewer disappointments resulting from thwarted expectations and better opportunities for accommodating different viewpoints.

FINDING COMMON GROUND

There are ways in which this can be done and ways in which it can be consciously or unconsciously avoided. It has become common practice for schools to develop mission statements. Though there are exceptions, this is often an exercise in creating an umbrella of platitudes so broad that everyone can rest comfortably under them — a process that painless seldom addresses real issues of contention. Yet it would be short-sighted to believe that such issues, centering on differing perspectives about how children learn, do not exist. Too often the administrative intent in all of this is to create the appearance of unity. What is sacrificed, however, is the articulation of a set of purposes that could help inform teacher practice and/or student behavior.

It is possible that the pursuit of such consensus regarding purpose is inherently divisive and should be avoided. In our experience the result is that the divisions remain and continue to thwart efforts to forge clear direction regarding the collaboration's intent. The enormous advantage we had at LAMS was that the collaboration began with the actual opening of the school. Lacking a prior history, there was far less resistance to the initial set of purposes that had been developed when the collaboration was planned. Our experience indicates that there is value in beginning with a staff that shares a common perspective. While it is not often an option, it would be enormously helpful if a teaching staff committed to the basic goals of the project could be recruited. In our case, the absence of a set of previously established organizational and operational modes was a distinct advantage.

An important finding of the study in Muncey and McQuillan (1993) was that articulating the philosophy of the school often ended up accentuating latent differences of view among faculty:

> The changes that occurred or were considered when a school joined the coalition forced the issue of what constituted the school's philosophy and revealed differences in faculty members' perceptions of their jobs, of the school's mission, and of the best way to educate students. As long as the school's philosophy remained unexamined, there was a fragile (usually unspoken and unquestioned) assumption that shared purposes, values, and beliefs underlay the everyday world of the school. (p. 487)

Such experience makes it evident that clarity, while both helpful and necessary, can produce division. One must choose where the greater danger lies. There is a corresponding danger, that of stating intent with such specificity that it ends up denying those working on the collaboration the flexibility they need to adapt to changing circumstances. As there is a foolish consistency, there is also an inappropriate specificity, one that demands rather than guides, limits rather than enables, requires response rather than reflection. John Goodlad (1994) states well the case for flexibility in a book on the theme of renewal when he suggests living with goal-free planning, action, and evaluation:

> Often, in fact, it is precisely as a result of activity that we become clearer about what we are doing and why we are doing it. Consequently, the world of human activity in and between education organizations does not lend itself well to concrete, sequential models of planning and evaluation.
>
> The subtitle of this lesson is "living with ambiguity," and our mentor is the organizational theorist, James March. For March, ambiguity is not a dirty word. Not only does he tolerate it, he embraces it. Closure *is* a dirty word.

Rarely is it ever achieved. In fact, if it is achieved, it is a good sign that either the issues are trivial or people are jumping to conclusions too quickly. . . . (pp. 110–111) (Emphasis in original)

One hastens to add at this juncture that clarity of vision and flexibility of response are not mutually contradictory phenomena. There remains a broad channel of purpose that can be navigated between the two by those intent on forging new directions. What must be avoided is, on the one hand, a rigid approach that seeks to replace ambiguity with an illusionary certainty and, on the other hand, the opposite extreme of conducting a project whose participants have no coherent sense of purpose or direction. The former is the more common problem for the everyday running of the schools and also for many college-inspired evaluative efforts. The dilemma posed by the lack of clear direction occurs with some frequency, however, and often goes unrecognized.

As we just stated, it has become common in education to state goals so broadly that they lack meaning. Staff no longer expect them to actually guide practice and so they are functionally ignored. In such instances, the effort to state objectives has been replaced by a tendency to state our deepest ideals. These may receive a certain level of surface acceptance, but they are far too vague or excessively idealized to actually guide behavior and are thus conveniently ignored. The project is then operating without a formal set of intentions but is functionally guided by an informal set of beliefs that has not been consciously articulated or discussed with staff. We note this as a danger, a problem to be avoided, without suggesting any specific remedies. That is a function which must be tied to particular projects, circumstances, resources, and available staff. What we point to is the need for both flexibility and focus. Collaborative agreements must reflect what is intended in ways that can serve as useful guides to behavior.

RECIPROCITY

In reaching such agreements, it is important that each of the collaborative partners insure that its own needs are met. It is our experience that the pursuit of mutually beneficial self-interest forms the most enduring basis for a collaborative venture. It is not uncommon for this principle to be ignored or given too little attention in the midst of initial enthusiams about forming partnerships. The schools have often served as hosts to college efforts from which they ultimately felt they received little benefit. Conversely, college staff have frequently overestimated their own staying power in proposing projects that they feel will "help" the schools.

One of the authors served as an evaluator on a major science project conducted by a large university in an urban setting. A number of the college staff committed themselves to working extensively in schools that had agreed to participate in the project. At the beginning of the process, when enthusiasm and expectations were high, college staff spent a considerable portion of their time at field sites. Over a period of several years, however, we noted a clear tendency on the part of that same staff to find their way back to the college. One could chart both the formal, highly heralded march out to the schools and the quieter, informal retreat back to the friendly confines of the college campus. Whether this was the pull of security (a return to a known environment) or mounting frustration about difficulties associated with implementation, it was clear that the college had miscalculated its level of commitment. We keep relearning Sarason's (1971) dictum that good intentions and missionary zeal are not enough to sustain reform efforts over time.

Developing organic relationships that will endure must be based on a skillful and objective assessment by each element of the collaborative about how their own interests as well as those of other partners in the effort will be served. Reciprocity is the key and it must be addressed early and reviewed regularly. Goodlad (1994) makes the point well:

> Because education is essentially a helping profession, the tendency in seeking a partnership is to do good. Yet relationships built on benign intentions tend to be fleeting. There is a greater potential in first seeing in the other partner a source of satisfying one's own needs. If there is a touch of cynicism here, so be it; but it is more a recognition of realities. And there is another important reality closely related: if in seeking satisfaction of one's own need, the needs of the partners are ignored, the partnership will soon dissolve. (p. 106)

That last point is important. It is mutually beneficial self-interest that we are suggesting. This implies a continual awareness of your partner's needs as well as your own and how effectively they are being served. It goes without saying that partners have similar responsibilities toward you. To aid this process, each member of the collaborative must assume the burden of informing others when their needs are not being met. This underscores the continuing need for dialogue. Projects must develop a sense of "we" through the continuous pursuit of objectives they have agreed are of common interest and concern.

These ideas form what are perhaps the key element upon which collaboration must be built:

(1) Avoid unnecessary specificity, some of which flows from fear of ambiguity rather than clarity of purpose.
(2) Form your agreements around a sound identification of shared interests whose pursuit will be mutually beneficial.

(3) Monitor and revisit early agreements or understandings to insure that their pursuit is not ignoring the needs of either partner.

USING DIFFERENCES TO GROW

Much is made of differences between the school and the college as institutions. This is as it should be, for the differences are substantive and present formidable obstacles to a successful collaboration. On the whole, however, these differences can and should be seen as strengths, as a positive rather than a negative. It is, after all, the differences that add dimension to the combined effort. Combinations of the same institutions (schools or colleges working only with their own) would present problems that are equally formidable and yet lack the added power that a broader range of interests, perspective, and experience can contribute.

For the college, one of the chief strengths of a collaboration with the schools is the opportunity it offers their staff to engage in "reality testing." This goes beyond the common canard that schools represent the "real world." The world each of us lives in is real enough (though different), and claims for a greater reality are generally an indirect way of saying, "You do not know my world the way I do." That is often true, but it is not necessarily the weakness some assume it to be. Outsiders are indeed blind to certain realities but quite observant about others. The key is to make effective use of what they see, rather than focusing excessively on their blind spots. The latter brings momentary satisfaction, the former can lead to productive ways to reshape your current "reality." That is true for both institutions. Part of the real strength they offer one another is that they do not see the other's reality with the same eyes.

Another strength is that the partner is not (at least initially) part of the social system. That often affords wider latitude for dissent and sometimes even gives these dissenting views a better hearing. To take advantage of such strengths, however, the partners must fight their way past stereotypes of one another that are common to their cultures. College staff often want to insist that schools are unnaturally resistant to change and hostile to external influences. That view could be more accurately applied to institutions in general and might also be seen as an asset as well as a liability, that is, not simply as a weakness that needs to be eliminated. Continuity within institutions is a by-product of this conservative tendency and serves a number of useful purposes. It can act as a counterforce to frivolous or meaningless change and prevent unnecessary disruptions in the way students and staff organize their efforts to pursue important goals.

There is a place for stability as well as change within institutions. The problem is that most have an inherent tendency to favor stability over change, even when it should be apparent that the former is stultifying or frustrating progress. An effective collaboration can be a useful mechanism for dealing with this tendency. By providing an outsider's perspective and an alternative view of process, the collaborator who is not part of the institution's internal organization or social system can be a source of support for necessary change. Thus, differences in experience, viewpoint, or need, if combined with skill and good judgment, can become the means through which collaborators offer one another the opportunity to change and grow.

One must note that this positive potential is not always seen or realized. It is sometimes difficult for outsiders not to fall into the role of respectful guests. This can result in a tendency to defer to the expertise of those most familiar with the basic conventions of the institution about what can be accomplished. This happened on numerous occasions with the schools. As noted earlier, a number of the recent studies of the schools that were highly touted (Carnegie Forum on Education and the Economy, 1986; National Commission on Excellence in Education, 1983) ended up putting forward some rather uninspired solutions. After concluding that the current state of education reflected a crisis, one such study included a recommendation for lengthening the school day and/or year. Such a suggestion seemed totally at odds with their own conclusions. Children educated in a system in a serious state of disrepair would hardly seem to profit greatly from spending greater periods of time in it.

The same can be said about recommendations to assign more homework or adopt higher standards. If the present system does not motivate students to work hard or do their best, how can such suggestions be expected to produce any real change? The mix of educators and people from the business world on various educational commissions and task force groups did not seem to result in producing recommendations for truly restructuring the ways in which students and teachers were to perform their roles. That may be an inherent weakness in the way such commissions conduct their inquiries. In the absence of a long-term partnership that would suggest, implement, and review the consequences of suggested changes, recommendations are made that produce consensus among members of the commission but often do not get to the heart of the problem. While collaborative efforts do not come with any guarantees, we believe they offer greater promise in bringing about change that is geared to the schools' specific problems. The willingness of collaborators to participate directly and provide resources to meet the challenges that result is an additional incentive. Sharing the burdens of success or failure has a wonderful tendency to focus concentration and temper excesses.

MAINTAINING THE VISION

The collaboration needs to be informed by a continuing vision of what the participants can accomplish together. In our case, the initial vision centered around the creation of an exemplary middle school that would serve as a model for others working in the urban environment. Once the school had been established along the lines contemplated, the task became one of making necessary changes or adjustment that would fulfill the best of the original vision while still maintaining a fresh perspective. For us, the path led to the creation of houses and interdisciplinary teams, a process that provided a strong sense of positive direction and a revitalization of the sense of purpose that had originally motivated the staff.

The challenge is a continuing one, however. As we have noted elsewhere, maintaining a sense of positive momentum requires effort. Schools do not maintain a strong sense of purpose unless the staff is engaged in an ongoing process of reflection about what is being accomplished and what improvements are necessary or possible. One of the primary strengths of school organization is the ability of staff to routinize process into procedures that no longer consume the time, energy, and thought that were originally required. This is an advantage that has obvious weaknesses, for it parallels a condition in economics known as the law of diminishing return. Up to a point, this routinization of process conserves time and effort, enabling staff to accomplish more because less conscious thought is required. Over time, however, the very fact that the procedures can be carried out without much thought gives rise to a rigidity born of a standard reflex. Thus faculty and student schedules, the length of periods, the approach to curriculum, or even instructional practices are all in constant danger of becoming hardened into routines that are given little thought and are subject to few changes. An essential part of an effective collaboration is to devote much time to avoiding the kind of stasis that arises when the reflective process gives way to these procedural rigidities. With that thought in mind, those responsible for our partnership again faced the issue of developing new goals for the future.

TESTING THE BOUNDARIES

Once the house plans and interdisciplinary teams had established their usefulness and were firmly in place, we returned to what we felt was the continuing challenge facing the collaboration. From the beginning, our underlying intent in forming the collaboration was to engage in a calculated process of boundary testing. Every institution has boundaries, limits that are placed on what are seen as legitimate functions for personnel or acceptable goals that the organization can profitably pursue. Institutions that share education as a common goal, like the college and the school, nonetheless maintain functional boundaries that act as real obstacles to greater cooperation. Sometimes the boundaries are useful and serve a clear purpose. In other cases, they may simply be the result of a lengthy tradition or unexamined assumptions about what works best. Our purpose was to examine these boundaries, to test the purposes they presumably served, and to challenge those that had little to recommend them. Our intent, where possible, was to create more porous boundaries that would facilitate an easier flow of human and material resources between the two institutions.

A NEW APPROACH TO TEACHER EDUCATION

What is implicit in this effort at creating porous boundaries is the belief that the removal of unnecessary, self-imposed limitations would benefit both institutions. What seemed clear to us was that an originally useful division of labor regarding teacher training (the college's responsibility) and inservice staff development (the purview of the schools) had hardened into a separation that benefited neither institution. It was our view that the schools could and should be more intimately involved with teacher training. Additionally, we were troubled by the way staff development had been separated from preservice training and the limited role assigned to the college regarding the latter activity. It seemed that a comprehensive strategy encompassing the two functions had much to offer to personnel at all levels in both institutions.

What we envisioned was a pilot project conducted at the school in which a cohort of undergraduate teacher trainees would be taught by teaching teams comprised of school and college staff. In our view, the purposes of staff development could be better accommodated by having inservice staff reflect together with college faculty about what constituted good classroom practice. Such an approach could better serve both the research needs of the university and the practical interests of those working in the classroom. It would provide practicing teachers with a forum for sharing both their concerns and their insights while offering college staff a laboratory site that would allow them to subject their views to the test of actual practice.

It remains our view that practicing teachers need opportunity for dialogue and reflection rather than the "training" that staff development so often implies. The model of bringing in outside experts to conduct workshop sessions is, from our perspective, both overrated and overused. While this approach remains one viable option, it needs to be combined with other techniques that provide greater potential for self-examination. Most staff development focuses too heavily on mere technique and ignores the more essential matter of changes in attitude and perspective that form the basis for more far-reaching change. And virtually all such staff training ignores school organization, assuming that changes in classroom practice can be accomplished in isolation, a belief rooted more in hope that in any objective assessment of how schools work.

Offering teachers the opportunity to translate their experience into terms that novice teachers could understand can be an effective means of promoting reflection. Working directly with these novice teachers in classrooms provides yet another dimension to that reflection, one that could easily lead those inservice practitioners to experiment with and revise current practice. Further, having the support of colleagues from the school and the college could help make this a team effort and greatly reduce the threat posed by attempts to implement new approaches. The frequent exposure to classrooms, students, and teachers would hold obvious advantages for college staff.

Our hope was that a number of the trainees could be hired by the school and thus become colleagues of the inservice teachers with whom they had formed a professional relationship. Further, the plan called for both the college and school staff to maintain continuing contact with those trainees who were hired by other schools. Part of the power of the model is the potential it offers for forming professional networks that support continued growth and reflection about conducting education.

REACTIONS TO A NEW MODEL FOR TEACHER TRAINING

Because we felt we had generally met the initial goals set for the collaboration, we now set about attempting to interest others in this broader vision of how the partnership might function. What we essentially proposed was a cooperative effort that included a role for the school in teacher preparation and an expanded role for the college in working with the school staff. It is an extension that has not been greeted with warm approval by either institution. The reasons for this are varied. Most are centered in the traditional separation of functions with which both institutions have become comfortable. The schools have remained focused on internal adjustments as the sole means of responding to whatever changes are demanded. While there is much talk of the need to improve the way new teachers are trained, the consistent assumption remains that this is the college's role.

The invitation to explore this possibility with some of the college staff has been greeted with interest, but little action on the part of school leadership. There is always greater concern expressed about how we are going to work with the school to improve its program and performance. Sadly, cooperating openly about the training of the next generation of teachers is not seen as a vital part of this process. Most of the energy continues to go into efforts to train current staff.

Part of the problem is that the training of new teachers is not viewed as being immediately helpful to specific schools. That makes it of limited interest to leadership at the building level. Leaders at higher levels are, at any given moment, committed to a variety of other broad goals that compete with such a proposal, and many of these are seen as offering more immediate benefits; nor have our colleagues at the college demonstrated any great desire to explore this as a possibility. Most remain satisfied with current practice, though there remains widespread criticism of its effectiveness both inside and outside the professional community. An additional impediment is that the effort we envision would require a long-term commitment, since it would need time to establish the necessary relationships and even more time before one could see results. Nonetheless, we believe the forging of a long-term plan for the initial training and the continuous development of teacher skills would help form a firmer foundation for the future.

FUTURE PLANNING IN EDUCATION

Perhaps it is precisely this orientation that has prevented the initiative from attracting much support. There is very little planning for the future anywhere in education. We do not anticipate teacher shortages well, do not take advantage of attracting quality personnel when there is a surplus, and do little to cooperate about shaping the future direction of the profession between the periods of recurrent crises we continually face. Over the long term, we believe the issue of attempting to make the boundaries between the college and the school more permeable is one that needs to be addressed, though not necessarily in the form we have put forward. Indeed, it is unclear at this juncture whether we will be able to attract much support for such a plan. The mixture of opposition and indifference, flowing from threat on the one hand and relative comfort on the other, does not bode well for its acceptance. We also recognize we are in danger of violating one of our chief tenets, that agreements between partners must be based on a perceived sense that the self-interest of both is being served. At the present time, there is not the feeling of urgency that would motivate broad segments of both communities to attempt the changes we are suggesting. Beyond that, there is the issue of finding the available time and energy for such an effort. We are suggesting significant changes in the roles of staff members who will be fully occupied with existing regularities during the period of transition. That is asking a great deal. Still, it remains our hope that a pilot project could be conducted in which those willing to take on additional responsibility could test the general feasibility of the approach. Should that not be possible, we will need to recognize that the effort is at least untimely, perhaps even ill-conceived, and we will consider new directions for the partnership. One of the nice aspects of collaboration is that bad or premature ideas stand a good chance of being rejected by either or both parties, a form of self-correction we do not always invite, but value highly.

CHAPTER 4

Stages of Development

Most activities that are not static, which have an inherent potential for growth and change over time, will evidence some pattern in the way their growth takes place. This is true of the activities of organizations which, like people, manifest stages in their development that can help interested observers anticipate and prepare for upcoming events. Our experience with collaboration, which has encompassed seven schools since the late 1970s, is that there are identifiable stages through which such partnerships typically pass. It is important to note that these stages are neither fixed nor invariant. The most one can say is that there is a reasonable likelihood they will occur and that, in most cases, they will follow a general order.[1]

As with developmental stages in other contexts described by Freud or Erickson, one cannot be certain progress will occur and it is possible to reach a plateau at any of the stages we have identified. Nor is the fact that such stages exist a guarantee that one will progress through them, smoothly or otherwise. The failure to recognize that there are such stages, however, may lead to unrealistic aspirations, unnecessary frustration, or premature acceptance of defeat when greater persistence would have meant success. Acknowledging their existence, on the other hand, can help to encourage other universities and public schools to initiate such partnerships with a greater awareness of the obstacles that must be faced. It would also arm involved staff with the kind of knowledge that might enable them to respond more effectively. Those engaged in collaborative efforts need energy, commitment, sensitivity, and good intentions to make them work. But they also need to anticipate the problems they may face. Knowing in advance that certain frustrations, delays, obstacles, or opposition are common can help one better prepare to deal with them. It can also help those involved to value patience and persistence, virtues whose importance are often grossly underestimated in preparing for such ventures.

Stage 1: Hostility

Almost without exception, the initial period in school–college collaboration is characterized by hostility and/or skepticism. School people have been made weary by experiences in which an "expert" from the university arrives on the scene, offers "solutions" to problems, and then quickly moves on. Further, they are wary of college professors who enter the public school world to conduct their research and then disappear to publish their findings in some inaccessible periodical. They do not want colleges to impose the very remedies that, many faculty members believe, failed to give them the practical preparation for their jobs in the first place. And it does not help that some of the most disparaging criticism of school organization and performance has come from the ranks of the college over the past several decades. It is an understatement to say that such an historical experience is not calculated to foster either acceptance or receptivity in the early stages of a school–college collaboration.

It is useful to admit and understand that there are forces working against the success of such cooperative ventures. They are not insurmountable, but must be taken into account, particularly at the beginning of the effort. Thus it is not unusual, perhaps even inevitable, that early on a teacher from the public school will ask a college professor, "When is the last time you were in a public school classroom?" The question, even when not asked directly, is always implicit. The presumption is that university representatives know little about the real world of schools. It is a view that has some basis in reality, one with which the college staff must contend.

Even where collaboration has been well planned and a broad segment of the school has been involved in preparations, such skepticism will remain. Personnel from the college must be prepared to demonstrate both their knowledge and its usefulness in a school setting. Until then, even in essentially cooperative settings, reservation will be the order of the day. And criticism is not always couched so obliquely. At a recent meeting exploring potential collaboration with a school district, a principal angrily remarked that he did not believe the college had much to offer him or his staff regarding the "practical" day-to-day operation of the school.

The extent of the hostility that colleges meet as they begin to work with public schools often depends on the conditions faced by the public school people. If each day in the public school is a struggle for order, and if teachers feel battered by frustrating experiences, then hostility is more likely than mere skepticism. If teachers feel patronized by their administrators, or if principals feel demeaned, unrecognized, or overly criticized by their superintendents, there is a good chance that the college may become the target of deflected hostility. But even with optimal educational environments and the best of intentions on the part of the college, most public school personnel will be skeptical at the outset.

Stage 2: Lack of Trust

While the tendency to vent hostility appears to lessen in intensity once a physical presence is established, lack of trust is not so quickly dissipated. The attitudes that form the basis for such a lack of trust are rooted in personal experience, as well as in the folklore of the school. Until such negative past experiences are countered by more recent successful ones and the stereotypes of college staff embedded in the folklore are challenged, there is little reason to expect change. Why shouldn't the teachers be suspicious of the professor/expert who arrives on the scene to head a staff development program conceived entirely by top-level administrators? Teachers often interpret this insistence by their administrators on staff development as a sign that their skills are felt to be inadequate and that they are in need of further education.

It is the one-sidedness of the view that offends many. Often finding themselves to be the subject of arbitrary evaluation and constant criticism, teachers can hardly be expected to feel grateful for the opportunity to receive "professional wisdom." As one such recipient said, "Why are we always the ones who need development? As far as I'm concerned, the ones who need improvement are the school administrators and the college professors who teach these meaningless courses."

The issue of trust is a critical one. A collaborative approach, by its very nature, affords many more opportunities for such trust to be established. It provides participants at all levels with numerous occasions where they can meet and share perspectives about issues of common interest. It is of great importance that opportunities are sought to interact on an informal as well as a formal level. While the formal meetings are the main means by which plans are devised and moved along, it is during the informal times that cooperative attitudes are developed, which can result in better refinements and broader support for the overall effort. The more extensive the dialogue, the greater the likelihood that it will reflect the real needs of participants. The opportunity for increased dialogue (both formal and informal) is one of the great strengths of a collaborative approach. This can be a slow process, but given time, patience, and good will, it is more likely that new attitudes will be formed, leading to improved cooperation.

Stage 3: The Period of Truce

Our experience suggests that when trust is confirmed, a perceived period of truce commences. In this stage, participants withdraw some prior negative judgments as the public school faculty members begin to sense that professors are not at the school merely to deliver sage advice but to learn and help. In order for that to happen, the college must carefully screen the staff it chooses to work in the collaboration. Personnel must be found whose true priority is to draw knowledge from the school setting and offer help to those who work in it.

Working cooperatively to address issues of mutual concern does help bridge the gap between the two cultures. We have found that antagonism diminished as professors and teachers worked together on issues important to them. These issues were defined on site by the people who were going to work on them. This mutual searching required a certain tolerance for "wasted time." It is always more expedient to define the needs in advance and then bring together people to work on the identified problems. The process we chose involved more floundering and some false starts, but ultimately it resulted in a clearer definition of problems and more productive working relationships. It also contributed to the atmosphere of trust. The college staff gained respect for both the difficult challenges teachers face and the hard-won skills they had developed over the years while learning to cope with their environment. Conversely, the public school staff found it was useful to have extra hands and an outsider's view of happenings within the school.

This time of truce is a necessary and delicate stage, one in which trust and mutual respect is gradually developed. It is important not to treat these valuable outcomes as incidental objectives, that is, as issues of less consequence that can be assumed or overlooked while the "real" goals of the collaborative are pursued. Trust and respect are the means by which any of the other goals will be reached, and it is critical that the importance of this process is appreciated and given the full attention it merits during this vital phase. Forging the collaboration is a key objective and it requires care, thought, and the application of resources.

Stage 4: Mixed Approval

At the next stage, school and college faculty members begin to gain each other's approval. This assumes, of course, that the initial three stages have been reasonably well managed. Bringing together people who have not worked with each other before always has an element of volatility to it. That is why, as we noted in the previous section, some considerable attention must be paid to the process. There is, however, one important factor for success in the initial stages of these collaborative ventures: People working together generally put stereotypes aside and try to find ways to work cooperatively. That positive disposition, combined with some good planning and effective support, can do much to get things moving in the right direction.

In our project, teachers began to feel enhanced by the college's presence. Professors provided another source of recognition through their words of appreciation and expressions of acknowledgment. A sense of being special surrounded the school as photographers or video technicians found their way to classrooms to document what was happening. A steady stream of visitors came to observe, and a number of newspaper accounts made note of the unique effort being undertaken. All this helped create a sense of positive momentum.

Further, professors who had learned how to work with teachers in a nonthreatening manner became advocates for the staff. They appealed for changes in school organization and provided practical and useful leadership in curriculum organization. By this time, those members of the college staff who had come because they had to fill out their schedules, had a research idea in mind, or had knowledge they felt compelled to deliver had either been screened out or departed, in frustration, on their own.

The school staff was also assuming roles at the college. All through the collaboration, the college sought opportunities for practitioners to teach graduate or undergraduate courses. As noted, the school principal joined the college staff as an adjunct professor. Some classroom teachers taught late afternoon courses in language arts, science, and mathematics. Other teachers were guest speakers in college classes or served on faculty committees. As roles merged, the opportunities for dialogue increased and people were able to communicate out of common experience.

Stage 5: Acceptance

By screening out uncommitted faculty, the collaboration often enters a period of stability, and the college gains acceptance, even admiration. When the Louis Armstrong faculty heard that the original agreement between the board of education and the college had been renewed, they broke out in spontaneous applause.

This is the era of good feeling. It is a time in which teachers, students, parents, community members, and college personnel believe that theirs is a good school. It is also a time in which professors and public school staff see the mutual benefits of the collaboration, and the idea of the school without the college involvement can become unthinkable.

With the passage of time it becomes clear that the development of a school–college partnership is a fluid process with no absolute endpoint. Changes are inevitable. Professors leave because they find the college's reward system does not recognize work in the field. The project's success opens opportunities in school administration, and a former principal becomes a district superintendent, an assistant principal becomes principal, and an administrative assistant fills a vacancy for assistant principal in another school.

We found that, almost overnight, the school was being run by administrators unfamiliar with the original philosophy of the school, unclear about the college's role, and lacking the sense of ownership that comes from growing up with a project. Other changes occurred: The support of top leaders in both the college and the board of education was lost as a new college president and a new chancellor for the New York City schools came on the scene.

Although it would be more comfortable if things remained the same, such personnel shifts are inevitable. Some of the energy that would normally be available for forward movement and strengthening of programs needs to be redirected into developing new relationships, orienting people, and restraining the tendency to return to the traditional patterns of running a school. This stage of acceptance may be mixed with a need to redefine priorities as these personnel changes force the leadership to reconsider what is possible and explore the potential presented by new staff.

Stage 6: Regression

Every project will sooner or later reach the stage where its productivity has peaked and the vigor with which goals are pursued declines. In this regressive stage, the original collaborative vision for the school may be blurred. This can be due to a variety of factors. Conditions may have changed so that the original vision is either no longer possible to reach or desirable to attain. New and more pressing challenges may have presented themselves, making the initial goals set for the project less important or as irrelevant by comparison.

It also possible for changes in key personnel to result in a diminished level of commitment to the earlier vision, forcing either a change in direction or the risk of an informal abandonment of the project's sense of purpose. Changes can also be forced by a less favorable match between goals formulated early in the collaboration or personnel currently available to implement them. For example, new administrators, accustomed to more bureaucratic approaches to supervision, may spark conflict by seeking to impose their will on a teaching group that has grown accustomed to more collegial treatment.

In any event, there will come a time when much greater effort is required, simply to maintain what has been accomplished previously. For those of us involved in the collaboration with LAMS, this was a time of discouragement and concern. It would have been easy to give in to feelings of pessimism about whether fresh energy could be found to acculturate new administrators and to find ways to reinvigorate the enterprise. It is a time when the collaboration can easily founder. Blind insistence upon continued pursuit of the original set of goals could be a disaster at such a juncture, and one can rest assured that there will be voices on both sides that will counsel just such a course of action. At this point it is critical for the leadership to provide opportunities for an objective assessment of where the project is and where it should be heading. The dilemma is that this must be done swiftly and, yet, in a deliberate, judicious fashion. Additionally, the assessment must be conducted while the staff is pursuing assigned tasks. These are not easy demands, but their very difficulty can serve to provide the energy needed to initiate an effort at renewal.

Stage 7: Renewal

In our case, Queens College faculty, aware that the project needed revitalization, begin to meet on a regular basis. We spent a full day at a nearby retreat center, identifying goals. The hours of interaction in a pleasant, informal setting, far from the interruptions and pressure of our normal job responsibilities, helped us to return to our tasks with renewed vigor and enthusiasm.

As with any project, one must periodically examine the need to shift focus, reorder priorities, examine verities. A point may come when maintaining momentum in the same direction can become a form of inertia. Our periodic meetings allowed us to entertain that possibility, and we concluded at two different intervals that efforts to renew the vision and move it to another level were necessary.

In one instance, the college and school staff met consistently over a one-year period to create a design for dividing the school into three houses. Each house would constitute one-third of the school population and would be directed by an assistant principal and assigned a guidance counselor. Teachers in the houses were formed into interdisciplinary teams who taught the same students and had joint planning periods built into their common schedules. The intent was to deal with the feelings of anonymity experienced by both teachers and students in such a large school by creating communities, building the informal and small in the midst of the large. We also organized a system of student advisories with no more that 12 students in a group. The plan was discussed with faculty several times during the year of planning, and was implemented the following year. Five years later, the changes remain intact — with the exception of the student advisories, which have become optional for the houses.

This effort clearly revitalized the collaboration, giving it new force and fresh energy during both the planning and implementation phases and in the period immediately following them. More importantly, it helped the school to move in a direction that was consistent with the ideals and vision that had been initially established for it.

Stage 8: Maintaining Progress

One of the key roles the college provides for the school is that it offers those within it an outside perspective about the nature of the activities in which they are engaged. From the inside, events seem to form into natural patterns that are either as they should be or, if not, must be accepted or endured. Those outside of the organization have the luxury of challenging those suppositions. Indeed, that may be one of their key contributions, and it can be quite useful

The college found itself having the same need. One of the things we lacked was an outside perspective about what we were doing and how well we were going about it. The school staff represented one useful source, but being caught up just as we were in the throes of the collaboration, they were not sufficiently disinterested to serve well in this role. We contacted consultants from other universities who shared their own explorations with us, and this did provide another perspective on our project. We also decided that each of us would keep a log of our experiences with a particular focus on key questions of interest. We met regularly to share perceptions in writing so that we could eventually produce material for dissemination.

While all this was useful, it was not completely satisfactory. The absence of an outside perspective regarding our activities, systematically offered by disinterested observers remains, in our opinion, a weakness in the collaborative model that we are employing. One way in which we have responded to this need is to attempt to bring new people into the college end of the collaboration as regularly as possible. That has helped to provide new energy as well as fresh ideas, and it has served to help us maintain progress. We recognize this is not a complete answer, however. The closest we have come to filling this void is during the brief period that the college provided us with Seymour Sarason's services as an outside consultant early in the life of the project. Once the collaboration was established, that role was dropped. It has, in our view, left a vacuum that remains unfilled. It is a service not commonly acknowledged as a need but one that is vital to any effort that intends to span a long period of time, such as ours.

Stage 9: Avoiding Marginalization

Over time it is clear that the college (or, we believe, any group external to the school staff) loses influence. The more personnel changes there are, the further away you get from the original group of collaborators and the looser the earlier agreements and understandings become. They are, in essence, renegotiated with each new leadership group. As educators have discovered through research conducted on innovation, there is no way to precisely replicate other efforts. In this context, earlier efforts become almost like a different project, negotiated with other people and with a separate set of implied understandings. Subsequent efforts are unlikely to duplicate either the understandings, the levels of commitment, or the early enthusiasm for the project. Hope and anticipation are powerful forces that give added leverage to initial projects and are not as easily tapped during renewal stages.

The primary danger is that the collaboration can drift into a school within a school mode, in which the partners perform their tasks side by side but quite independent of one another. It is easier for subsequent leadership to find comfort in this type of an accommodation. It removes a certain level of tension inherent in working as partners. but at the cost of seriously reducing the scope and depth of what can be accomplished. If care is not taken, the college can be reduced to a provider of services which are fed into the ongoing bureaucracy in ways that the organization sees as least disruptive. The price of such comfort is the loss of any potential to address recurring problems in anything other than the normative fashion. The collaboration, if it is to maximally benefit both parties, needs to find ways to resist such tendencies.

Stage 10: Reestablishing the Mission

This is a deeper level of development. It is neither a set of specific activities nor simply an effort to review the goals. It is an attempt to redefine the broad purposes of the collaboration, to see afresh what we can do and how we should function as a joint project. It is like renewal, but on a total project level and it would be better viewed as if it were a new beginning. Renewal is searching for particular issues, programs, or themes we can improve upon. Reestablishing the vision involves reexamining the philosophical perspective that informs the choice of activities in which the project will engage. This is a stage that cannot be reported on at this time, since it is a process in which we are presently engaged and have not fully experienced. We are reasonably confident, however, that collaborations which last long enough will eventually come to this point. What is examined at such a time is not program but purpose, a vigorous review of the very notion of collaboration and what it can continue to accomplish.

WHAT WE HAVE LEARNED

We know now — as we could not have known at the beginning — that when a public school and college work together, the process is one of constant change. Some teachers retire or go on sabbatical; others transfer into the school. Curriculum mandates are hurled at the school from state and city agencies and budget support varies with a fluctuating economy. The attempt to control every detail of the project is like trying to bottle a cloud on a windy day. It is clear that a collaboration moves through different stages of development, and to ignore them is to invite disappointment, frustration, and possible failure.

We have also come to know that school–college partnerships can succeed, that public school personnel and college faculty can indeed develop effective approaches to education together. We have seen how collaboration has kept professors' views of education fresh by maintaining linkages with children, teachers, and schools. Theory and practice have been more closely connected, teachers and professors have become less separate, and all of us have been reinvigorated by the chance to make a difference in schools.

Forging such a collaboration entails both the willingness to accept risks and the ability to bring together disparate elements and form them into a purposeful whole. Those involved in initiating a collaboration face formidable obstacles. An earlier review (Trubowitz et al., 1984) of the problems we encountered while initiating a collaborative venture in another, completely different setting, is illustrative of the types of difficulties that must be faced at the beginning: "Few projects have the luxury of time in which to plan initial activities properly. Most move from the stage where energies are thoroughly consumed in efforts to have the project accepted to one in which that battle is won but the program must begin immediately. Little time is left for planning a smooth entrance" (p. 137).

Later efforts to maintain the vision often bring one back to some of the same difficulties encountered at the beginning. One of the chief problems is finding the time to reflect and carefully plan for new directions. As the example just cited makes clear, those involved in such projects are beset by the dual difficulties of gaining acceptance for a comprehensive plan while simultaneously managing elements related to implementation. The metaphor we have chosen to describe this dilemma is that of attempting to repair the engine of a car while the motor is running. Most innovation conducted in the schools is like that. The system is generally in full operation while the planners are attempting to make adjustments in how it is running. What this often means is that some elements cannot be dealt with at all (e.g., union contract considerations, bus schedules, length of the school day) while others can be worked at only with considerable risk (e.g., redefining tasks, changing assignments). As with a running engine, there are parts you simply cannot touch lest you risk incapacitating either yourself or the motor. With a school, as with an engine, the elements that present themselves as most easily accessible are often those quite peripheral to the basic operation of the system. One can end up working on what is available rather than focusing on where the problem lies. On the other hand, planning that takes place apart from actual functioning can often be unnecessarily protracted or result in an unrealistic sets of goals. The effort to properly integrate planning and implementation is a major dilemma for those involved in collaboration. The problem is exacerbated during revitalization because the regular program must be attended to while one is also attempting to institute change within it.

Another major difficulty that must be contended with is changes in the leadership of the school. Such changes have huge import for the future of the collaboration. It is common for new personnel to lack commitment to the original goals of the project. Not part of the initial planning, they arrive with no sense of ownership regarding its primary purposes. That is quite natural and to be expected. What we have found, however, is an increasing unwillingness on the part of new leadership to consider that anything done prior to their arrival has real worth or meaning. Most seem excessively committed to making their own mark and this often translates into disparaging or ignoring earlier efforts. We have labeled this the B.C. (Before the Change) syndrome and it is a problem that is increasingly prevalent. It is characterized by the spoken or implicit sentiment: "But that was before I was here."

In a culture already accused of historical amnesia, this leadership trait only exacerbates a tendency that is already problematic for the schools. Most innovation is attempted with little or no reference to past experience with the same or similar ideas. That tendency combined with the B.C. attitude on the part of new administrators only compounds the strains imposed on the collaboration, since no prior effort will receive strong support until it can be redesigned in that individual's image. Changes in leadership will come and they will not usually present difficulties that are insurmountable. However, they can represent major challenges, such as that exemplified by the attitude that what is useful is synonymous with the arrival of new leadership.

SUMMARY

We believe Stages 1 through 6 will be commonly experienced by most of those involved in collaborations. Many such efforts will not survive the sixth or regression stage, where a real effort at revitalization is needed. The remaining stages pertain to collaborative efforts which manage to survive over an extended period of time.

Consideration of that element of time, the issue of having the collaboration endure, has led us to adopt the concept of dieting as a model for change. We have found it helpful to view the collaboration the way a thoughtful dieter would view the issue of weight loss. An examination of research regarding the loss of weight would reveal that it is far easier to shed excess pounds than it is to keep from reverting back to the weight at which you started. Similarly, we have found it is far easier to initiate collaborative efforts than to sustain them. It is maintenance that is the key and not the initial flurry of activity and effort that receives so much of our attention.

This is not to say that either weight loss or initiating collaboratives is easy. The point is that they must be considered as merely one stage in an ongoing process and not necessarily the most difficult one. It is a mistake to place excessive emphasis or expectation on that one stage at the expense of later ones. Maintenance is the critical phase and it often requires far greater thought and effort than it is given. That unfortunate truth seems lost on many dieters and some proponents of collaboration. Energy, resolve, and effort are often "front-loaded" and there is not enough staying power to sustain whatever advantages have been won.

If the intent is to make any change that has been attained permanent over time, then one must give careful thought to the efforts that must be made to maintain it. There is a need to recognize, in diet as in collaborations, the apparent disposition to return to an earlier stage of equilibrium even when there was considerable lack of satisfaction with it and much hard work invested in moving beyond it. As the preliminary study on the Coalition of Essential Schools has concluded (Muncey & McQuillan, 1993), there are no quick fixes or miracle cures. Maintenance, then, becomes a critical factor to consider in the planning and implementation of any collaborative venture.

NOTE

1. Some of the ideas presented in this chapter first appeared in an article written by Dr. Trubowitz (Trubowitz, 1986).

CHAPTER 5

Predictable Problems

The attempt to link two different cultures, college and public school, might be compared to an effort to mate two different species. The joining will be difficult and obstacles will be inevitable; this was the case with the Queens College — LAMS collaboration. Although we set forth on our collaboration with the Board of Education aware that all would not be smooth, we did not pause to list the problems that were likely to occur as we worked with people and groups whose ideas and backgrounds were so different from our own. We just plunged ahead, fueled by a desire to put into practice our vision of good middle school education. Our experience has indicated that there are predictable problems a university will encounter as it works with a public school. We have experienced the difficulties inherent in any attempt to introduce new educational approaches. We have faced the periodic need to establish new relationships as project personnel changed. We also have a deeper understanding of the nature of the divisions that exist between college professors and public school staff in their views of education, their norms of behavior, and their knowledge of each other's institutions. We have seen impediments caused by the impersonal quality of bureaucracy and the blind imposition of regulations. We can bear personal witness to the problems that arise as a school grows in size.

Although awareness of these problems prior to launching a collaboration may serve to forearm the participants, we would also point out that to dwell on them at too great a length may serve to discourage rather than to inform. A case can even be made that our failure to focus on *all* of the problems had some benefit. The words of John Schlesinger (1994) in *The New Yorker*, commenting on his ability to produce the film *Midnight Cowboy*, illustrates the value of not anticipating every possible problem: "Lack of knowledge is awfully freeing. It gives you the strength to overcome obstacles — obstacles you're not fully aware of until later" (p. 42). In retrospect, we believe that our quick immersion into the collaboration allowed us to keep our idealistic, and perhaps extravagant, conceptions for the future. We did not begin by laboring over potential problems. Rather, we reached agreement on common purposes and hurled ourselves into the project.

All of this is not to make a case for ignorance, but to underline an understanding that although problems will occur, they need not lead to inaction and inevitable failure. Indeed, our entire thrust is that those involved in collaboration need to exercise a combination of preparedness and flexibility. There is a danger in structuring things too tightly, where not enough allowance is made for staff to learn and grow. Care must be taken not to screen out the intuitive through excessive ordering of events and overplanning. At the same time, however, the staff must be reflective and always trying to anticipate problems by remaining sensitive to developments and where they may lead. A great help in this is an awareness of past history (our own and that of others) regarding what problems are likely to arise.

We believe that one must begin with the understanding that each collaborative venture will present its own specific set of challenges. These will emerge out of the particular set of circumstances and people involved in that project. We also believe, as we noted above, that there are some predictable problems, situations that are generic to the collaborative effort and which have a high probability of occurring. These are likely to include, though they will not be limited to, the following items.

CHANGES IN LEADERSHIP

The most significant problem we faced in our collaboration is represented by changes in leadership. As much as we would have liked the people in charge to have remained the same, in a school–college venture that extends over a period of years personnel changes will occur and there will be a need to adjust to differences in personality, administrative style, and attitude towards the collaboration.

Seven Principals

From the start we knew that key to the success of the collaboration was developing a good relationship with the principal. We wanted the head of the school to see us as allies rather than threats. Foremost in our minds was consideration of how to provide support and enhance administration, and the need to tread carefully the line between making suggestions and seeming critical. We wanted to infuse sound educational practice into the school while remaining sensitive to the personality and philosophy of the school leader. We anticipated that it would take hours of attending meetings together, sharing ideas, co-presenting at professional conferences, and co-writing articles before suspicion would give way to acceptance, and acceptance could become trust.

Experimental projects draw attention and heighten visibility for its participants. The collaboration provided a special opportunity for individuals who sought to make a contribution, try something different, and enhance their reputations. One result has been that the principalship of LAMS has attracted candidates who were upwardly mobile. This has provided the project with able leadership, but has also led to a high rate of turnover. Since its beginning in 1979, the school has had seven principals, with some moving to superintendentcies and others to posts in suburban schools. Although we expected some change, we little realized that there would be a need to consistently adjust to so many different personalities.

Since each school leader brought a different administrative style and a different perspective to the position, our mode of interaction in each case was different as we tried to be sensitive to the needs and concerns of the new administrator. The influence of the college in the collaboration was highly dependent on the status of the relationship with the principal and the frequent personnel changes presented a constant challenge to a sense of continuity and purpose.

As college liaisons, we were not alone in dealing with periods of uncertainty. The teachers, too, had to find ways of interacting with each new administrator. Questions arose in teachers' minds: Would she/he provide the same level of support given by the previous principal? Would a particular approach gain approval or criticism? Would she/he be effective in creating a school tone conducive to learning?

Professors also felt themselves thrust into limbo. With each change in administration they wondered if their research projects would be allowed to continue. They questioned if there would be understanding and recognition of what had been previously attempted and accomplished. There was concern about the part they would continue playing in school decision-making.

Eight Chancellors

The collaboration has been taking place in what had been named "The Chancellor's School" because of the unusual nature of its origins. Any sense of ownership by the chancellor, however, came only in the first years of the collaboration. With every succeeding chancellor, interest in the Queens College–LAMS project diminished, and seven chancellors later we faced the ongoing problem of explaining the existence of the collaboration to the powers that be at Central Board of Education headquarters. We realize now that it would have been unrealistic to expect continuing close involvement of the chancellor's office, since running the New York City public schools is such a massive venture with so many other activities to occupy the minds of school leadership. We did not anticipate, however, that we would have to review the history and purpose of the collaboration with every subsequent change in administration. We have found that with every new chancellor we've been asked such questions as, "What is the collaboration?" "Why hasn't there been competitive bidding so that a different college could be involved?" "What is a college person doing chairing the school-based management team?" Such questions indicated how the lack of a sense of ownership has resulted in ignorance of the origin and direction of the project.

Four College Presidents, Four Deans

College leadership, too, has changed over the years of the collaboration. We lost a college president and dean of the school of education for whom the collaboration was of highest priority. Their immediate successors supported the collaboration but from a distance and with only occasional encouraging words, a style quite different from President Cohen and Dean Lidstone, both of whom regularly visited the school and consulted about problems and progress. The absence of the original sponsors of the collaboration demonstrated for us the meaning and value of support. The constant interest and involvement of a president and dean stimulated effort that went well beyond what might be expected. The school filled our every discussion; we were constantly thinking of it. There was a tenacious continuity of attention. The result was a group that worked both nights and weekends.

The support we received gave us the courage to take risks and to try new ideas. It enabled us to resist any violation of the original agreement. It helped us to feel part of the mainstream of college activity. It permitted us to direct all of our energies toward working with our public school partners rather than bringing college authorities along to our point of view. There was additional backing forthcoming as steps were taken to modify the college reward system by giving credence to work in the field for purposes of tenure and promotion. The loss of input from a president and a dean made it more difficult to find the power to sustain forward momentum.

Both the roles and the attitudes of those who fill them continue to change. The most recent Dean of the School of Education, Ron Yoshida, has once again become a strong supporter of the collaboration. He visits the school regularly and offers strong, consistent leadership regarding the details of the collaboration. The dilemma is that this increased support has been offset by reductions in funding and the rapidity of changes in leadership that the school has experienced. The latter circumstances result in a loss of momentum that increased commitment from the college end alone cannot correct.

The frequent changes in school leadership have had the effect of adding layer upon layer of insulation between the early history of the collaboration and current circumstances. It seems likely to us that this must eventually result in an almost total disconnection from the initial set of goals. The difficulty is that the continual changes also mitigate against reordering priorities and establishing a new direction for the collaboration. This poses a dilemma for which we have no clear solution.

The problem has been compounded by the changes at higher levels of the college and school bureaucracy. As the original supporters of the project slowly disappeared over the years, we have found it more difficult to be involved in key decision-making. With a diminished access to top leadership, we have been obliged once again to working our ideas through levels of the bureaucracy, a time-consuming and frustrating process that is common to urban environments. It is doubly hard, however, for those with no status in the bureaucracy.

In any collaboration sustained over a period of time, there will be personnel changes. It is the task of project leadership to seek ways of preserving institutional memory so that positive elements of the partnership are not lost. Such changes also require those who continue to work in the collaboration to overcome the frustration and irritation they feel as, again and again, they face the responsibility of forging new relationships, promoting continuity of effort, and maintaining a sense of progress.

RESISTANCE TO CHANGE

Those of us involved in collaborations need to be reminded that when change is introduced in schools there is a need to take into account the inclination of staff to keep doing that to which they are accustomed. The tendency to change as little as possible prevails as efforts are made to modify existing practice. Thus it was not a source of complete surprise for us to encounter resistance as we sought to implement a vision of middle schools that ran counter to traditional practice in New York City schools.

We believed in heterogeneous grouping, not tracked classes; we saw value in nongraded classes, not groups organized by age; we wanted flexible scheduling to avoid fragmentation of learning, not education bound by 42-minute segments. We imagined a school constantly involved in a process of self-examination, always seeking improvement, and not a school whose main focus was the maintenance of the status quo.

As we have noted elsewhere, it was probably because the college's role was deemed so essential that school administration went along with our views. Classes were organized on a heterogeneous basis and interage groups were set up. Departmentalization (scheduling of 42-minute periods) remained, however, as the principal, his traditional secondary school background firmly ingrained, manifested a great deal of discomfort with any suggested alternatives. Over the years, numerous other bureaucratic impediments presented themselves. College promotional practices resulted in denying us access to professional staff. At the school, issues like seniority rules (both formal and informal) frustrated efforts to place skilled personnel in key roles. The fact that school staff are largely appointed by a central bureaucracy rather than the principal added to this problem, as did a later policy of transfer rights that allowed senior teachers from other schools to displace younger staff. Urban education, squeezed between the conflicting demands of the school and union bureaucracies, presents many challenges to those attempting to improve the education of students.

We soon discovered that breaks from traditional practice are not easily accomplished, even within cooperative settings. The presumption that teachers would be able to work comfortably and effectively with heterogeneous, interaged classes proved wrong. We were asking teachers with little experience in working with students of diverse ability to deal with an unfamiliar class composition. Since teachers found the nongraded aspect of classes most daunting, we retreated from this view and classes were reorganized into age groups. We learned from direct experience that there was a lag between the generation of new educational ideas and the ability of teachers to deal with them.

We remained steadfast about heterogeneous grouping, since we considered it an essential element of effective education. This decision raised problems. "Teaching to the middle" and reliance on a single textbook represents prevailing practice in many middle and junior high schools. In elementary schools the approach most often used is to segregate the verbally talented into special classes. The result was that some teachers and parents complained that the needs of all children were not being met and bright children, in particular, were not being challenged. The concerns of parents were exemplified by the mother who said, "If I had kept my child in the neighborhood school, he'd be in a special class for the gifted getting an enriched program. Here he spends most of his time helping other children."

We found that implementing heterogeneity involves more than student assignment to classes. We took on the continual task of helping teachers deal with the reality of students of different abilities and work with parents to have them see the value of mixed classes. Despite the difficulties, there has been success in that teachers have developed a variety of instructional strategies, and the large majority of teachers and parents have been won over to the concept of heterogeneously organized classes.

As we tried to move the school toward the implementation of house plans, interdisciplinary instruction, teaching teams, and an advisor/advisee system, we have encountered once again the complexity of the change process. We experienced anew the fact that most teachers prefer the stability of traditional practice to the uncertainty of educational innovation. In the process, we learned to respect teacher resistance to change as a caution not to attempt too much too fast. We have found that sometimes the appropriate tactic is to retreat from actions implemented if receptivity has not been established. We also had to deal with our own resistance to yielding even temporarily on beliefs we held about education until there was greater teacher readiness to accept and implement such ideas.

We have become more aware of how unrealistic it is to expect all teachers to move in particular directions solely because it seems educationally desirable to do so. We have learned that in the process of introducing a new instructional approach to one group of teachers, one result may be that those not involved will look askance at the innovation, since they feel implied criticism for not moving in the recommended direction. And we have been confronted again and again with the reality that collaboration involves ongoing problem solving, including the need to deal with continual resistance to different educational approaches. It is clear that the gap between vision and implementation is not easily bridged, but we have also been affirmed in our belief that — with persistence and patience — forward movement can occur.

DIFFERENT VALUE SYSTEMS

The history of school–college collaborations gives reason to expect that in any such arrangement conflict between the participants is predictable. When people have different values, when they have had different experiences, when their actions are motivated by different goals, and they are subject to different pressures, there will be periods of misunderstanding and suspicion.

Different Views of Education

The collaborative venture began with a series of meetings with Board of Education representatives to develop a design for the school. We saw

quickly that differences in values would be a problem. The board representatives wanted the school to give special emphasis to skills. Most reacted with patronizing tolerance to the college's proposal that the arts have
equal status to other subject areas. There was an underlying antagonism
to the "ivory-towered" professors who knew little of the practicalities of
schools and the political realities of urban education. The majority of
board officials believed in the status quo, for what existed was what they
had created. Theirs was a world of prescribed lesson plans, developmental
lessons, aims written on blackboards, and a system of rewards and punish-
ments based on administrative approval and disapproval. At various times
during the collaboration, some board personnel reacted with disbelief to
the idea that teachers would make contact with parents and outside groups
without approval from the principal, that teachers need not submit detailed plan books each week for administrative inspection, or that formal
classroom observations may have limited value. For the most part, such
ideas were viewed as issues that had been decided, not topics open to
discussion.

Different Views of the Role of Parents

Other value differences caused conflict throughout the collaboration.
Some teachers and administrators were wary of parent and community
involvement, viewing such involvement as intruding on professional prerequisites. As one administrator put it, "I've had 35 years of experience
and I'm not going to have any parent telling me what to do."

Another example of an attitude which saw parents as outsiders was
the instance in which an administrator reprimanded a teacher for discussing school problems in the presence of a parent at a school-based management team meeting. The incident illustrated a view of parents as outsiders
rather than as potential partners who were entitled to share in the problem-solving process, a perspective that essentially negated the need to
have parents on the committee. These are views that are deeply embedded
in the culture and are not easily changed.

Different Views of the Teaching-Learning Process

Value differences made for different responses to recommended changes
in teaching approaches. The attempt to make an advisor/advisee program
an integral part of the school illustrates a divergence of educational view
that likely represents the norm at most middle schools. No one, it seemed,
disagreed with the idea that getting to know middle school students as
individuals was desirable. When it was proposed that an advisor/advisee
program would be an excellent means of achieving that end, different

forms of resistance manifested themselves. There was the teacher who said, "Giving me an extra group violates the union contract. It's another period to teach."

Another remarked, "An advisory group means four teaching periods in a row. I can't handle that."

Still others simply expressed their unwillingness to participate. Some in this group saw advisories as antithetical to their usual teaching approach, while others felt discomforted by the prospect of working in a more personal manner with youngsters.

The result of these differences was that the effort to have the entire school participate in an advisor/advisee program faltered and only some staff members agreed to work with small groups of youngsters.

Middle schools are particularly susceptible to varied views of the teaching/learning process. Teachers prepared to teach a single subject at the secondary school level often differ in approach from elementary school-trained instructors, who are more likely to focus on the individual. It is probable that this schism between a subject-matter emphasis and a child-centered approach will continue until we have preparation programs specifically designed for middle school teaching.

We have seen that only the naive would envision a school where teachers represent unanimity in their educational philosophy. There will be differences and to expect unity in educational perspective, especially in school systems where the choice of teacher candidates is restricted by union regulations, is unrealistic. An acceptance of the reality of differences need not mean an acceptance of the status quo. For despite value differences, school and teacher growth can occur if premature judgment gives way to an ability to listen and understand the other person's position. It is possible, for example, for a teacher who evidences no interest in students and whose total focus is subject matter to be effective with students. It can happen that a teacher who is uncomfortable with parents connects with youngsters. An important part of the challenge is to forge these very differences into a cohesive whole that continues to meet the primary goals of education, albeit in independent, unique ways. That is more easily spoken of than done, but it remains the best way to maximize the talents of a varied staff.

LACK OF A UNIFIED EDUCATIONAL PHILOSOPHY

A Different Way of Looking at Problems

Other conflicts will surface as professors and public school personnel interact, since each has learned to deal with problems in different ways. Public school staff, unlike college faculty, feel pressure to find quick solutions. A result is that they often approach problems as though each has but one cause and one remedy will suffice to erase the difficulty. For example, an administrator maintained that the problem of deteriorating student behavior would disappear if teachers and administrators would stand in hallways as students moved from class to class. When it was suggested that, in addition, it might be useful to look at the problem more broadly and explore other possible reasons for deviant behavior, the impatient response was "We don't have time to get into philosophy." The fact is that time for reflection is not readily available in the maelstrom of activity in a school of 1400 pupils. College professors, on the other hand, have time for thinking and discussion built into their schedules. For them, the process of problem solving is not driven by the need for an immediate solution.

The questions raised by the identification of school tone as a problem are convoluted and difficult. They can not be resolved by refusing to deal with them. In this instance, as on other occasions, professors and faculty lined up on opposite sides, with the school becoming fixed on finding the short range answer and college faculty calling for a more reflective analysis of problems with the aim of discovering more long-lasting solutions.

The college staff assigned to the school had the benefit of prior public school experience. This background allowed us to recognize that some problems demand an immediate response and, at the same time, to urge exploration of other ways to deal with difficulty.

The differences in approach to school problems illustrate the ongoing tension between a need to react quickly and a view that calls for thinking, gathering data, and discussing. This struggle produces benefits as well as conflict since it sensitizes college staff to the pressures on public school staff and presents teachers and administrators with another vision of how schools can operate.

The Benefits and Drawbacks of Experience

The fact that teachers rely exclusively on personal experience to guide their beliefs and actions often leads to a rigidity of approach. For example, those who have worked only with homogeneous classes often see ability grouping as the preferred form of organization. It goes without saying that experience provides powerful and important support for decision-making. The negative aspect of teacher experience is that it occurs within a confined environment. This limited exposure provides limited data. The result with regard to class organization is that some teachers reject the findings of research that point out the positives of heterogeneous organization and report no special value to homogeneous classes. In some cases teachers react with anger to the professor who initiates a discussion with the words "Research tells us . . . ," for they interpret these words as a downgrading of their personal experience. There is also a problem in that this phrase is often used far too casually and indiscriminately to support cherished beliefs about how schools should function. The "research" cited, when it actually exists, is often not all that clear.

Insularity of approach comes from being too closely involved in the operation of an organization. The problem for all participants in a collaboration is to go beyond personal experience. We have found that one way of gaining objectivity and perspective is to locate an informed, perceptive external person and to be open to the observations that may be offered. We have also seen how prior experience has caused teachers and college staff to view authority in different ways. Public school people reared in a staff-line bureaucracy are sometimes reluctant to question administrative decisions. College faculty who are accustomed to exerting influence on hiring, granting of tenure, and other decisions often see this as teacher passivity or as excessive deference to administrative authority. The larger truth is that most of us see one another through the lens of our personal experience.

Different backgrounds make for different kinds of behavior. But despite the occasional clashes caused by these differences, collaborative efforts nurtured by time and patience can bring positive results. Indeed, they can serve to help us broaden our perspective about what is possible within our own institutions.

GAPS IN KNOWLEDGE

There is much that college faculty and public school personnel do not know about the operation of each other's institution; the result is that they become frustrated when requests are not honored. In our collaboration, ignorance showed early. When teachers were to be hired for the school, some professors recommended their star graduates for positions. They were unaware of the need for teacher candidates to have New York City licenses. When these recommendations were not followed, these college faculty reacted negatively to what they saw as unnecessary red tape. In another instance the principal asked that college faculty assigned to the school punch a time clock as did the teachers of the school. His request showed his lack of understanding of a college culture that provides autonomy and activity unbound by the demands of a clock. The school system eventually eliminated the time clocks for its own staff, thus moving in a direction this administrator would not have thought appropriate.

Unrealistic expectations came from other misconceptions. The public school staff imagined that the college had unlimited resources, little realizing that the university had its own budgetary limitations. Initially, there was also the belief that within the college faculty were any number of available professors who would help provide suggestions that might functionally eliminate some of the school's ills. This view attributed an omnipotence that was unfounded and demonstrated a lack of awareness that finding college faculty who were willing to work in the school is hindered by a college reward system that does not credit work in the field. Such a view also reveals a curious paradox: College faculty are disliked for unfounded assumptions about their level of expertise and yet are also looked to for miracle cures.

Public school personnel look at the life of a college professor with envy. They see a relaxed approach to time with no apparent pressure. They do not see a culture based on a need to publish. Although college instructors are not bombarded by the exigencies of day-to-day operations, they do feel an omnipresent urgency to write for publication.

College faculty with the luxury of time have sometimes been put off by teacher reluctance to attend meetings beyond the school day. As professors became part of the school, they learned how physically and emotionally draining a teacher's life is and how unreasonable it is to demand additional hours from people already stretched to the limit.

PROBLEMS RELATED TO SCHOOL SIZE

Growth in school size is an important factor too little considered, for the larger the unit the more complex the problems. As the school increased from 150 pupils to the present population of almost 1400, it became more difficult to develop and maintain the support of the various constituent groups. In the beginning communication occurred through face-to-face talk. Sharing of ideas was constant — over lunch, in hallways, at social gatherings. With the expansion in the number of staff have come feelings of separateness. There are people in the school who don't know each other. Large school size has caused informality to give way to formality. Written reports of meetings have now replaced verbal exchange as the major means of disseminating information. The widening scope of responsibility for principal and college leadership alike has made it impossible for them to get to know all the children and adults. Many have become shadow figures whose ideas, concerns, and feelings remain unknown.

We have seen that lines of communication have lengthened and interaction has become less personal. We have focused much of our effort in recent years to deal with this change by working toward the development of schools within schools and teaching teams. We also spend a great deal of time wandering the building, listening to teachers, offering recognition for achievement, and sharing ideas. We strive to diminish the effect of large school size by supporting advisory programs and hosting breakfast and lunches for teachers in the interest of expanding opportunity for interaction. The size of the college as an institution is also a problem. Here too the lines of communication lengthened as changes in the original leadership denied us direct contact with higher levels of the college administration. The problem of size is never confined to physical dimensions or the numbers of people involved. One needs to take into account the implications size has for depersonalizing the project, complicating the lines of communications, and introducing disillusionment by making progress too distant or difficult to see. We believe projects should be small enough in scope for those involved to have a reasonably clear idea of their central purposes and whether they are making progress in attaining them.

UNION CONTRACTS AND BUREAUCRATIC FIATS

As noted earlier, the provisos of union contracts give rise to other problems. For example, assignments to certain out-of-class positions are dictated by contractual prescriptions with the result that seniority rather than superior qualification becomes the factor deciding selection. In other instances, teachers who had received unsatisfactory performance ratings have been able to transfer to Louis Armstrong. It needs to be recognized that a public school–college collaboration operates within restrictions and the stipulations of union contracts may inhibit total freedom in teacher selection and assignment. A task of project leadership has been to work in cooperation with union representatives to maintain and upgrade the skills of teaching staff by increasing opportunities to grow and work together cooperatively.

In any large system there will be times when directives are delivered from the central bureaucracy that show a complete ignorance of the school. On more than one occasion we have needed to remind the board that they were contemplating moves that would violate the original agreement between college and public school. There was the time officials were preparing to transfer an additional 150 pupils into the school and ignore the understanding that there would be a cap on the school's population.

After some wrangling the idea was put aside. We needed periodically to resist proposals that stemmed from ignorance of the project.

Bureaucracy presents further difficulty as it seeks to impose control from a distance. For example, the mandate of the State Department of Education for accelerated classes in the eighth grade interferes with the goal of heterogeneity. Staff development becomes sterile and mechanical when Board of Education officials from afar prescribe a specific number of observations for each teacher to be recorded on set forms.

THE FALLACY OF THE QUICK FIX

Another problem comes from the expectation that a collaboration between public school and college will bring immediate results. Collaborations succeed by dint of hard work, ongoing attention to problems, patience, and persistence. Successful collaboration is achieved with time and only after problems are overcome. In addition, in any collaboration there will be setbacks. Part of its strength is the type of tension it creates by introducing competing ideas into the system. These can result in rich opportunities for learning and significant achievement. Results will not come overnight and very often they will not come without some cost in difficulties that need to be overcome.

EVALUATING RESULTS AND ANTICIPATING PROBLEMS

The issue of assessing and anticipating the results of initiatives put forward is critical to success. Most of the resources of any large organization are expended on maintaining ongoing operations. There is little time or energy, and even less inclination, to examine how well the various functions are being performed. It is even more rare to assess how similar attempts have fared elsewhere. Thus, for most schools, reviewing ongoing efforts or trying to anticipate difficulties receives far less thought than they deserve and programs suffer accordingly.

What seems to characterize attitudes in this regard is the conventional wisdom that says, "If it ain't broke, don't fix it." This is a view based on an underlying truth. It also masks an underlying fiction. If all maintenance were treated in such a way one would wait until a home had a fire before considering having the chimney cleaned. Some effort needs to be put into anticipating problems if major difficulties are to be averted.

We tried to encourage a proactive stance and avoid what we called "red light" maintenance, a view based on the notion that the red light in the car will tell you when you need to add oil. The guiding philosophy behind that approach is to wait until the problem announces itself before taking remedial action. That is not always wrong. It can be a useful technique. The problem is that in some cases irreparable damage can be done before one is aware that steps need to be taken. Sometimes it is simply wiser to try and anticipate problems by looking at where and how they have occurred elsewhere in similar circumstances. In this regard we found it consistently instructive to consult the experience of others working at various forms of collaboration. This proved helpful, particularly in the early stages of the partnership when mistakes could prove costly, but it is good practice throughout for all aspects of the school program.

It remains true that assessment, in general, receives far less attention than it merits. One of the absences we felt most acutely was that there was no funding specifically designated for program evaluation as opposed to operation. We attempted to make up for this lack by employing a variety of formative evaluation techniques, but the absence of a systematic review denied us valuable input.

SUMMARY

This identification of problems is not meant to discourage prospective collaborators but rather to encourage a realistic outlook. A collaboration between a college and public school will produce some conflict, but it can also bring rich learning and significant achievement. At Louis Armstrong we have seen that "problems come with the territory." We have also seen how productive collaborations can be, and that is why we openly embrace their potential and encourage their use.

The main purpose of this chapter was to attempt to help others prepare for the type of problems that are likely to occur. In that vein, we want to offer an important caution: We speak of predictable problems so that they can be better anticipated, not because we believe they can be avoided. We note these potential difficulties so that when they occur, those involved do not feel they have failed or are experiencing a phenomena totally at odds with the process they have adopted. If the collaboration lasts a reasonable period, those involved are likely to confront most of the issues we have raised. Too often participants tend to review lists of problems like these and conclude that because they have been identified they can either be eliminated or reduced to the status of a minor inconvenience. That would be a dangerous illusion. We accept the principle that to be forewarned is to be forearmed. We also know from experience that being forearmed will not exempt one from dealing with some very thorny problems. That is why our advice is not to adopt a strategy that attempts to circumvent the difficulties, but one that prepares and sustains the participants as they attempt to resolve them.

Students at Louis Armstrong Middle School helped their art teachers create this mural near the front entrance to the school. Among the Queens landmarks shown are the Queensborough Bridge to Manhattan, the Unisphere from the 1964 World's Fair, Shea Stadium, the TWA terminal at Kennedy Airport, and the Queens Hall of Science.

A close-up of the mural at the school's entrance.

Turnover at the top has been a recurring problem. Shown here *(foreground, left to right)* are the late Joseph Barkan of the New York City Board of Education; Saul Cohen, the former President of Queens College of the City University of New York; Anthony Alvarado, the former Chancellor of the New York City Board of Education; and Al Herman, the former Principal of Louis Armstrong Middle School. Shown in the background behind Saul Cohen are two former Presidents of the school's PTA, Luisa Di Nenno and Leon F. Payne, Jr.

Anthony Alvarado, the former chancellor of the New York City Board of Education, visited the school in 1985.

New York State Assemblyman Jeffrion Aubry speaking at the 1987 dedication of the Louis Armstrong mural at the school. Assemblyman Aubry was a community youth leader at that time. Also shown are *(far left)* the late Lucille Armstrong, wife of Louis Armstrong, and *(left)* New York City councilwoman Helen M. Marshall.

Participating in the memorial service for Lucille Armstrong were Walter Jackson *(left)* of the school's custodial staff and special education teacher Gwendolyn Moore.

Physical education teacher Nina Chakrian took a five-year family care leave from the school, but returned in 1996.

Continuity of adult involvement at the school has been an important factor in student success. Shown here are two former interns who remained at the school and now teach sixth grade, Susan Howard-Bubacz *(left)* and Lisa Braunstein.

Shown from left to right are Rossana Perez, another former intern now teaching sixth grade; Sid Trubowitz, Director of the LAMS–Queens College collaboration; Donna Somers, a former intern and teacher who has moved to Boston but remained in contact with her colleagues, and Susan Howard-Bubacz.

The school has its own museum. Shown here attending its Louis Armstrong exhibit is Professor Jimmy Heath of the Aaron Copland School of Music at Queens College.

PART III

THE COLLABORATION
What We Have Learned

CHAPTER 6

School–College Relations

THE SCHOOL AND COLLEGE WORKING TOGETHER

We've been at the school since 1979. Parents, teachers, administrators, and local residents (including politicians) see us as much a part of the institution as any other member of the school community. We go to school parties, attend parent–teacher meetings, participate in staff conferences, function as members of the school cabinet, serve on the school-based management team, and interact with staff in hallways, the dining room, and in the library. It is taken for granted that the names of college personnel belong on the organization sheet, on mailboxes, and on school stationery. There is agreement that Queens College is integral to the operation of the school.

A recent event produced an example of how ingrained in the life of the school is college participation. The previous principal had announced that she would be leaving to head a middle school in a suburban community. Concerns about what would happen followed this news. Uncertainty regarding the quality of leadership a new principal would bring filled the minds of many. Parents and teachers alike came to the director of the collaboration and in almost plaintive tones asked, "You and the college will be here next year, won't you?" It was a request for stability but it was more. It was an affirmation of the benefits that have accrued as a result of the collaboration. It was a statement of the belief, as one parent put it, "that the college is the school and the school is the college."

At the college, there is acceptance of the fact that the LAMS–Queens College collaboration has brought credit to both institutions. Each year at the school's graduation exercises, the college president speaks glowingly of the "best middle school in New York City." The LAMS has become a place for college students to do field work, for student teaching, and for professors to send their own children. The school–college project is regularly included in a listing of the university's accomplishments. While the college may not be lavish in its practical support of the collaboration, the leadership clearly sees its advantages.

The development of our school–college relationship didn't simply happen. Like a good marriage, it resulted from ongoing interaction in which the partners exchanged mutual respect and each one added to the strength of the other. It came from the ability of the participants to weather the ups and downs of changing circumstances. It emerged from a shared understanding that final success is not the aim — rather, the goal is commitment to the idea of continuing growth. It happened because those most intimately involved didn't allow problems, expected or unanticipated, to cause them to give up.

In the beginning there was lack of trust. Public school staff were distrustful of the college's intentions and concerned about the tendency of its staff to honor the theoretical over the practical. Indeed, they were leery of college faculty offering any help, for these were the people who had failed to give them practical preparation for their jobs in the first place. College personnel, too, viewed the collaboration with pessimism. They were skeptical of our belief that we could establish a relationship where failure was the norm. Part of the problem was the fact that the memory of another school–college relationship (noted in Chapter 1) was fresh since, just three years earlier, the college and another school had severed a collaboration leaving a legacy of venomous antagonism that exists to this day. Others expressed caveats directly. One said, "I hope there are a lot of easy exits out of the building." Another said, "There had better be a lot of security guards around." The consensus was that we were naive, idealistic, and unrealistic. Perhaps we were. If we had taken a great deal of time to ponder past experience, the likelihood is that we would not have had the gumption to embark on a relationship where frustration and failure were considered likely results.

But a few of us felt the need to move from the isolation of the college campus into the real world of schools, and we were exhilarated by the challenge of doing something significant, working with public school administrators and teachers, and creating a good middle school.

PROFESSORS

The key to any progress that has been made are the people who have chosen to lend their talents to the effort. There are the professors who have so woven themselves into the fabric of school operation that their presence is taken for granted. They move in and out of classrooms and among children as would any teacher in the school. This integration into the school came only with time and it took professors who could establish themselves in a nonthreatening manner and avoid a "we-are-the-experts" stance.

We have found that it takes a special kind of college faculty member to move into the public school scene. Such individuals must possess a combination of interpersonal skills, professional competence, and the ability to seize opportunities when they are offered. A collaboration also calls for people who are ready to take risks, and to expose their ideas to the test of reality. It needs people who see the possibilities for carving out new areas of knowledge by working with teachers and students in the schools. It asks for people undaunted by the time and effort needed to develop relationships. Teaching a course on campus entails far less energy.

The Queens College collaboration has been supported by a number of people who view themselves as doers, who recognize that public school teachers represent a resource, who cannot imagine themselves working in a professional education program without the benefit of a laboratory site, and who see the need to connect their college courses with the real world of schools.

The development of a cadre of productive college personnel did not occur instantly. At first, there were some professors who accepted assignment to the school and proceeded to project superior airs, to question the value of the collaboration, and to focus on things to criticize. There was the college faculty member more concerned with publication than with contribution, who developed a monograph claiming results as if from a large-scale experiment, when in fact it was based on activity with only 11 teachers. There were others who complained periodically about the principal's administrative style and looked to us to correct his faults. There were still others who failed to fulfill their obligation when teachers gave them less than a warm welcome. It became clear that faculty who were to work in the school needed to be chosen more carefully, and that expression of interest and the ability to work in the field were essential. The professors who experienced and expressed an undue level of frustration were soon moved to different assignments.

The collaboration has profited from the presence of a number of professors who, over the years, shaped a university existence combining work in the field with their role as college faculty. We offer the following examples of the experience of several of these successful staff members in order to demonstrate the potential advantages of a collaborative approach. We wish to emphasize, however, that this work is not for everyone. There were college staff who found the role incompatible with their personal needs, others whose contribution was too limited for them to continue, and still others who found the trade-off in time worked too heavily against them. Success in such endeavors is a highly individual matter, but when it occurs there can be wonderful outcomes for all involved.

Fran Curcio

Fran Curcio, a professor of mathematics education, has been a participant in the collaboration for over 8 years. She represents a professorial model that illustrates skill in working with teachers, an ability to find in the school material suitable for publication, and success in merging preservice and inservice education. Her words (Curcio, Perez, & Stewart, 1994) illustrate her manner of interacting with teachers:

> I did not want to impose myself on any of the mathematics teachers, and I certainly did not want anyone to feel threatened by my presence. I was interested in learning *with* and *from* my middle school colleagues, but I was not sure how I could communicate this to them. I found one teacher who expressed an interest in working with me. Our relationship began when I told her that I could bring some manipulative materials from the college. Doing so made me popular among other teachers who were looking for a way to obtain materials. As a result, I was welcomed into other classrooms. For the most part, I became an extra pair of hands, working more like a student teacher or an assistant teacher than as a college professor, but I didn't mind. Gradually, after several months I felt comfortable suggesting that we try something a little different — introducing a nontraditional, nonroutine "problem-of-the-week" that we would assign to the students and ask them to work on for a week before discussing it. This proved to be very successful, and the problems found their way into other teacher's classrooms.
>
> A lot has happened to me since these early days — I have learned so much about the daily realities of the classroom and I have experienced the joys of watching students constructing and discussing mathematics. Working at the Louis Armstrong Middle School has been a highlight for me during my tenure at Queens College. (pp. 206–207, emphasis in original)

In Fran Curcio we see key descriptors for the role of field-based professor — helpful, nonthreatening, open, collegial. The validity of these adjectives is supported by the comments of two sixth-grade teachers who wrote:

> We believe that at least two elements have contributed substantially to our successful school–college partnership: willingness to work together based on a respect of ideas, and trust built on an openness to discuss problems, difficulties, and misunderstandings. We experience these elements as we continue to collaborate on mathematics curriculum and staff development projects. The willingness to work together has developed because of a genuine interest in learning and sharing that the teachers and the professor bring to the collaboration. The college faculty member has helped us to build our confidence by respecting our ideas. We are not afraid to say, "I don't know." We do not feel threatened by Fran because she learns from us just as much as we learn from her. When we are involved in team-teaching with her, we enjoy the give-and-take attitude that develops between us and

among the students. Our questioning techniques have improved, our understanding of mathematics has been strengthened, and our interest in mathematics has blossomed.

Presevice education and inservice staff activity most often operate as separate components of teacher development. Dr. Curcio has blended these two aspects by having undergraduate students work with small groups of children under the supervision of three middle school teachers who, in turn, are guided by a college professor. The children provide the undergraduates with experience that reflect the realities of the urban school. Not only do the undergraduate students grow in their understanding of learning styles, of how to develop basic skills, and ways to make mathematics successful, but the mentor teachers also learn from the experience. After each session with the children, the mentor teachers join with the college professor and the undergraduates to discuss observations, recommendations, and suggestions. At this time, the undergraduates are able to question the teachers about how they evaluate student progress, how to manage the use of manipulatives, and how they manage learning centers and cooperative learning groups. Mentor teachers, in their new role of clinical professor, grow in understanding as they respond to these questions and interact with the professor. The undergraduates have attested to the value of this approach: "The middle school teachers helped me to understand and appreciate the kinds of knowledge I will need to be an effective teacher." "This was a true methods course—the combination of theory and practice was truly rewarding for me."

Dr. Curcio has helped the school's mathematics teachers broaden their professional community. She worked with several teachers to submit an application to participate in the Middle Grades Mathematics Project Professional Development Teams Workshop at Michigan State University. As a result of the school's selection, teachers have had ongoing interaction with a national network of mathematics instructors. They have conducted workshops for teachers, made presentations at professional conferences, and co-authored articles for educational periodicals. Dr. Curcio's focus on doing has not impaired her ability to reflect on several questions designed to refine and enhance what we do as professionals. Collaborative projects are providing data to describe the effects of small group interaction on the development of problem-solving skills and how students communicate mathematical ideas by representing information in visual displays.

Our collaboration has illustrated the development of a new kind of college professor, one who is a combination of classroom teacher, researcher, facilitator, networker, and colleague.

Linda Catelli

Physical education programs in public schools have low priority. They are viewed as the place to alleviate staffing problems by scheduling large groups of children with minimal teaching supervision. Erroneously labeled as "gym" classes, they are thought of as a frill rather than an essential program. This attitude results in programs that are primarily focused on recreation rather than on curriculum designed to achieve objectives based on students' motoric and health needs. LAMS has, over the past 15 years, benefited from the presence of Linda Catelli, professor of physical education, a field-based professor who has fought the tendency of schools to give little value to physical education. She has become the advocate for sound instruction in physical education. The teachers have found in her a spokesperson, and, with her support, physical education has been elevated to an area of importance.

Dr. Catelli has done more than serve as the missionary leader for a point of view. She has helped physical education teachers to feel a greater sense of professionalism as they have taken over responsibility for the supervision of student teachers and have joined with her to co-author articles. Dr. Catelli bridges the gap between theory and practice by teaching a preservice course entitled *Orientation to Teaching* at LAMS and then providing the college students in her class experiences in the gymnasium with the physical education faculty. She has been able to introduce a "new" physical education into the school with greater emphasis on health, fitness, wellness, and motor competence for ensuring a healthy and active lifestyle. Along with the physical education faculty she has designed an action research study to assess individual and group change in health-related fitness performances of a selected LAMS student population. She and her physical education colleagues have visited other places to disseminate what they have learned. They regularly present their findings at national conferences and have been working with other schools to help them launch wellness programs.

Dr. Catelli represents another example of a professor who has brought teachers a sense of professionalism, who has contributed to the effort to integrate preservice and inservice education and who has, at the same time, derived great satisfaction from her research and her success in program development.

Regina Krummel

The collaboration has brought to college classes a reality they never had before. Typically, if you're a professor planning to teach a class of 30 sophomores preparing to be teachers of literature, tradition would have you meet the group on campus, assign stories to be read, and deal with them in class discussions. Regina Krummel, professor of English education, found a different way. She concluded that prospective teachers might best get to the essence of stories about adolescence by sharing reactions to what is read with a group of 13- and 14-year-olds. This view led to the formation of a combined class of college sophomores and eighth graders at LAMS. For over 10 years this kind of group has been taught by Dr. Krummel and two eighth-grade teachers, Bert Honigman and Nancy Rosenthal. The eighth-graders and college students react to the same short stories and the prospective middle school teachers learn first-hand about the ideas and feelings of boys and girls who are like the pupils they may one day be teaching. The middle school students see other norms of behavior and thinking as they interact with the 19- and 20-year-olds.

The experience has proved valuable for the professional staff as well. Nancy Rosenthal, eighth-grade language arts teacher, describes what the opportunity to work with Dr. Krummel has meant to her: "Working with Regina made me realize what a burden it is to be in a classroom all by yourself. It's stimulating to hear another point of view. Having another adult in the class allows me to take time to observe the students, to see them from a different vantage point." Dr. Krummel too reacts with enthusiasm to the combination class. She says: "Our collaborative journey becomes an adventure, as we continue to examine our reaction to the students with whom we work (college students and early adolescents) and elicit from them their responses. Each group learns so much from the other."

Combining eighth-graders and college students in a class on adolescent literature illustrates how useful it can be to break down the barriers of age in forming learning groups.

Robert Edgar

For the first 7 years of the collaboration Robert Edgar, professor of social studies education, showed how he influenced teachers by becoming part of the social existence of the people with whom he interacted. Professor Edgar worked with a group of veteran teachers who could be described as individuals who had learned to deal with day-to-day responsibilities in ways that avoided severe problems and who felt little need to modify their approaches. He overcame their suspicion of "newfangled" methods and ivory tower types to become their friend and colleague. He had an exquisite awareness of what to do in working with teachers and what to avoid.

We quote from an interview with Dr. Edgar published in our first book (Trubowitz et al., 1984) which illustrates his sensitivity in dealing with teachers:

> One of the things that I had personally found difficult is the need for college professors to constantly reinforce their superiority to what they see in existence in the school. I found that a nonproductive attitude because teachers responded with "We are in there actually engaged in the schools and you are sitting on the sidelines and telling us what to do and you have not earned the authority to do that sort of thing." The consequence is this maintenance of the gap between the two. (p. 160)

His skill in working with faculty is demonstrated by the following statement:

> How do I think I motivate people? By being responsive to their ideas, by encouraging them when they have them, by trying to work out ways of participating with them in their ideas and inevitably being influenced by my own ideas, by trying to conjoin my ideas with their ideas. (p. 160)

He points out the importance of relationships in achieving change when he says:

> Most of the time in education you don't talk about the change in teachers that comes about when they feel that somebody is attending to what they are doing and therefore makes them feel that the profession is more rewarding to them. Teachers are very isolated creatures, and I do think that we have to build in opportunities for professional-social kinds of relationships that will keep them stimulated. (p. 163)

Professor Edgar died this past year. An indication of the degree of his acceptance as part of the school is the recent decision by the school staff to present an award for outstanding achievement in social studies in his name. The comments of Jeff Arkin, a social studies teacher, who presented the first certificate in Dr. Edgar's name, show school–college interaction at its best. He said, "When I began as a new teacher 13 years ago, I faced many difficult questions. How would I fit into the school? How could I best make a contribution to our students' education? Where were my career and life heading? Bob Edgar helped me answer these questions. He became my colleague, my mentor, and my friend."

In his years at Louis Armstrong, Professor Edgar became part of the social studies faculty. He was indeed a member of the group he helped.

Other College Faculty

Other professors have survived the test of time as well, with relationships that continue to flourish. For over 10 years, Dr. Lee Ann Truesdell has filled the dual roles of mentor for a group of special education teachers and researcher. She has taught courses at the school, led summer workshops, and worked with administrators to implement organizational changes.

Dr. Harry Rice, professor of social studies, was part of the collaboration from the beginning. His presence in the school went beyond working with social studies student teachers and faculty. He also participated in school-management meetings every week at 7:30 a.m., attended special Saturday sessions, appeared at open house recruitment evenings, and even led an early morning bridge group for youngsters.

In Dr. Rice's role at the school we see a modification of the usual approach to student teaching supervision. Instead of simply visiting the school to make a few observations during the semester, he was there each week to provide ongoing consultation for students and cooperating teachers.

The school-college collaboration at Louis Armstrong has achieved a long life in large measure because of a group of college faculty who have continued to make working at the school a regular part of their professional lives. Many of this core cadre have had extensive public school experience, with the result of identifying with the life of teachers with whom they work. These professors enjoy being in schools and recognize the need for ongoing experience in the field to keep themselves and their courses current. They have been willing to give time to this effort and have succeeded, in most cases, in accommodating to the college's criteria for promotion by writing about the results of their exploration into school life.

Additional Personnel Resources

Over the years the college was able to bring in a number of outstanding educators who served in roles that made them widely available to school staff. In particular, we want to take note of the important contributions of four individuals.

Dr. Monroe Cohen served the collaboration in a variety of capacities. In the early years he organized a highly successful adult education program for senior citizens that brought many outstanding speakers to the school. He also served as the editor of a number of publications produced by teachers and college staff including occasional papers dealing with classroom instructional strategies, a regularly published newsletter highlighting the collaboration's activities, and a series of monographs on issues of educational interest. Beyond this, Dr. Cohen also served as our first formal intern supervisor and began the process of refining the approach that we employed. He brought to each of these roles a passion for excellence, a humane concern for students, and a rich and varied background as an educator.

Dr. Wilma Heckler was the first person we employed to specifically oversee the internship program. She brought to this task great intellectual energy, boundless enthusiasm, and the capacity to inspire the best from those with whom she worked. She was a force for good educational practice, not only for the interns, but for many veteran teachers at the school, who learned to trust and respect her ideas. Dr. Heckler's educational perspective was rooted in a solid background of experience. She had worked as a classroom teacher, educational consultant, and college instructor. More importantly, her reflections on these experiences had allowed her to form a powerful vision of what education could be at its best. She was a potent resource for the interns and the school staff.

John Melser followed Wilma Heckler as the intern supervisor. He had a unique background: He began his professional endeavors as a teacher in his native New Zealand. In time he became the supervisor of teachers in a large educational region and then moved on to become a college teacher. John eventually settled in the United States and, after a brief period of college teaching, he was selected as the principal of P.S. 3 in Manhattan, where he served for 18 years. He brought this fine background of experience, combined with powerful intellect, to his role in the collaboration. John was a formidable thinker who had a gift for encouraging others to reflect about what they were doing. He was provocative, thoughtful, and extremely knowledgeable. He filled the assignment perfectly and maintained this effective dimension of the collaboration. He was a force for good educational practice in the school.

Richard Lewis, a renowned poet/teacher, has been with the collaboration for 15 years. He brings a unique perspective to education as he helps children and teachers utilize their imaginations and recognize the value of playing with ideas. He introduces the expressive arts of writing, painting, clay modeling, and movement in an enjoyable, meaningful way. Each year the children with whom he works produce booklets of poetry and contribute artwork for a museum exhibition.

ADMINISTRATIVE LEADERS

Another significant factor in the development of the collaboration was the support of top leadership—its value cannot be overestimated. Chancellor

Frank Macchiarola of the Board of Education saw the college as a strong ally in the creation of an exemplary middle school, which would attract a population to meet the requirements of a legal decision mandating an integrated student body. The effort was also greatly aided by Saul Cohen, President of Queens College, whose view of the university's mission included strong support of teacher education and a continuing outreach to public schools. The presence of these two institutional heads provided practical assistance and psychological sustenance. President Cohen's ongoing interest in the collaboration and his recognition of its importance stimulated even greater effort on the part of those who were involved; these professors felt increased status on campus because the president constantly referred to the achievements of LAMS. He also delivered the message that work in the schools would be considered in tenure and promotional decisions. Those of us who labored at the school to implement the collaboration no longer felt isolated from campus life. The backing of the chancellor and the president lent weight to our concerns when problems arose — we could raise issues and feel confident that they would be given attention.

Of great importance also was the fact that the collaboration had allies in the Dean of Teacher Education and the Chairperson of the Department of Secondary Education, both of whom were fully involved in the collaboration. They were partners in the exploration of ideas and gave the project help in finding appropriate faculty to serve in the school, in smoothing the way to tenure and promotion, and in easing scheduling problems.

The support of top leadership launched the collaboration from a position of strength. We could forcefully put forth our views on heterogeneous grouping, which allowed us to overcome the objections of traditionalists who saw us as naive theorists. We gained some leeway in the hiring of staff and were not obliged to develop a faculty made up solely of teachers on transfer. We had the ear of a principal who saw us as equal partners in the formation of policy. The compatibility of self-interest of the chancellor and president generated enthusiasm, energy, commitment, and optimism. But such commitments do not last forever. With changes of leadership have come changes in the level of support. The need to adjust to these changes began early and has been both extensive and ongoing.

Since the birth of the collaboration, there have been eight chancellors, seven principals, four college presidents, four deans of education, and six Board of Education superintendents with direct responsibility for the school. A child with that number of parents would likely show confusion; the results for the collaboration have been similar. Elements of the original mission have been lost and we continue to strive to recapture them. The search for positive change has met obstacles that, as we look back, were inevitable in the face of the number of educational leaders whom the collaboration worked with.

The frequent changes in leadership have led to diminished interest on the part of those in charge. It has proved difficult to transfer a sense of ownership to succeeding leaders. The message communicated is "What I didn't create, what doesn't have my imprimatur, doesn't receive my full commitment." New leaders are anxious to make their mark. Most do not believe that successful projects started by others will redound to their benefit as will activities they inaugurate.

Another result has been that visits to the school by the chancellor and the president, once common, have not taken place in recent years. No longer are there meetings with Board of Education representatives to discuss the progress of the project. For the Central Board, the school has assumed a paradoxical position, as a source of positive publicity for developing a center of effective education, but also as a nuisance when parents of children not admitted to the school badger the authorities for a reversal of the negative decision. At the college there is less mention of the collaboration's achievements.

Those of us who are at the school day-by-day, week-by-week, feel a sense of being out there on our own, thinking, strategizing, and working to function in the most effective way. We experience the loss of a place to share our concerns, get help, gain perspective, and be recognized. But, as directors of the project, we continue our efforts to reach optimum effectiveness. We seek others to reflect with, for we feel the need for an outside, neutral pair of eyes to help us see things that too close an involvement in the project causes us to miss.

The absence of interest has been manifested in ways that go beyond the loss of support. It has affected how staffing the school has occurred. After Saul Cohen's administration, work in the field has brought no recognition in terms of tenure or promotion at the college. It has become more difficult to recruit new professors to the collaboration, for there is reluctance to take time from individual research to serve in the school. The Central Board, with diminished involvement in the collaboration, has used the school to make assignments of convenience. Several assistant principals were transferred to the school based on decisions that seemed more relevant to the needs of the broader educational bureaucracy than those of the school. Little or no attention was paid to the work being done at LAMS or the skills that were needed to accomplish it. Each of the individuals assigned brought their own individual strengths and a background of prior experience in administration. What they didn't bring were comparable views of middle school education. The result was an administrative staff representing conflicting perspectives. When the principal sought to introduce an advisor/advisee program, her efforts lacked the support of an assistant principal, who had an opposing view of how to deal with students.

The examples of garbled philosophy emanating from administration were many, but suffice it to say that school leadership operated like a large orchestra headed by four separate conductors: Discordant sounds were inevitable and the sense of mission was clouded. We were faced with the difficulty of trying to maintain progress in the absence of a unified vision about our central purpose.

The attempt to promote good middle school education was complicated from the start by the issue of what constituted the school's philosophy. There were differences in faculty members' perception of their jobs, of the school's mission, and of the best way to educate children. The mixture of secondary school subject matter teachers and elementary school licensed staff made differences inevitable. Despite these problems, with a unified administrative group and college staff, it was possible to take steps in the direction of middle school reform. When the philosophical conflicts among the administrative staff became apparent, the task of implementing change grew more problematic. Efforts to move teachers towards curriculum modification, house plans, advisor–advisee programs, and interdisciplinary instruction resulted in even further division among faculty. There were those who believed in the middle school philosophy and sought to implement learner-centered instruction in keeping with the needs of 10- to 14-year-olds. There were also those who felt that fundamental changes in school structure or teaching practices were not needed. As some recent research has indicated, implementing innovative ideas can result in exacerbating differences that would otherwise be glossed over.

Each new principal brought his or her own view of administration and the college's place in the conduct of the school. Some exhibited a great reliance on college recommendations; others sensed the integral role filled by the college and, at the same time, resisted sharing their decision-making powers; still others communicated the view that the college had little part to play in organizational decisions and professors and interns were there to provide service. There were also those who enjoyed the dialogue with college personnel, who began to see themselves as part of a "thinking team," and who recognized that making decisions together could result in self-enhancement rather than a diminished strength.

Collaboration implies ongoing conversation about key issues in the school. The opportunities for such interchange have been many and are available to this day. The college director of the project participates in the administrative cabinet, where important matters are discussed. With the advent of a school-based management team, it was the college director (Dr. Trubowitz) who was selected by teachers and parents to chair the sessions. Every meeting of the Parents Association Executive Board and the general parent population finds the college director reporting on university activity at the school. Most important have been the informal discussions in the principal's office, at the college, and on trips to professional conferences. Decisions regarding staff hiring, new programs, proposals for organizational change and professional development have been products of varying degrees of shared thinking. The extent of the college's role as partner continues to be dependent on the attitude of the principal and of how he or she perceives the place of university involvement.

The arrival of each new administrator initiated a new feeling-out process. The metaphor some of us used was the Waltz — the beginning of yet another polite, wary dance in which one must demonstrate the ability to keep in step and yet maintain a proper distance. One must again offer assurances that the college is in no way attempting to aggregate power: We seek to provide support. We hope that in time, no matter what the initial stance of the principal, that the message that we can be of help as collaborators in the operation of the school is received. Every change of administration calls upon us to exhibit patience, persistence, and understanding. It demands from us a willingness not to succumb to frustration for having to go through the same process so many times.

It has become evident that if collaborations are to be sustained, the problem of succession of leadership needs to be considered. Is there some way of transferring a sense of ownership from one leader to the next? How can new leaders best be oriented to the mission established for the collaboration? Are there ways of ensuring that leadership personnel overlaps from one administration to the other? To whom does the responsibility belong for informing and educating newcomers regarding the collaboration's purposes? Is there some way of establishing for one and all times the college's role as collaborator and not simply as a service provider?

In the initial stages of the collaboration (a "feeling-out" period for all the participants), the support of top leadership was crucial. After 17 years and a history of mutually beneficial activity, the college's role has become institutionalized and the collaboration survives, despite the absence of deep involvement of chancellor and college president. The college remains an integral part of the school's operation even as principals come and go, but maintaining consistent levels of success makes increased demands upon time, energy, and skills.

OTHER ROLES FOR TEACHERS, ADMINISTRATORS, AND PROFESSORS

Another step in the direction of gaining mutual confidence was the sharing of experience. We were ever alert for opportunities to have administrators, teachers, and professors shift roles. From the outset the design for the collaboration included having the school principal join the college staff as an adjunct professor. Teaching a college course brought administrators to campus, where discussions before class in the dean's office gave opportunity for reflection and countered the feeling of aloneness that is the plight of school principals. As one principal put it: "The guy in the field has an enormous sense of isolation. We don't get to talk about education, about conceptualizations, about ideas. You get locked in to the day-to-day operations. It's too easy to become a paper pusher and a number manipulator. I feel the colleagueship tremendously. It's been a growth experience on a professional, personal, and human level."

Teachers too were recruited as instructors for late afternoon courses in language arts, science, and mathematics. We developed a different approach to student teaching supervision with experienced classroom teachers assuming responsibility for this task. Conference presentations by professors and teachers became a normal mode of operation. College faculty and school personnel have also cooperated on writing articles for professional periodicals. In addition, we initiated a series of occasional papers in which teachers described unique classroom activity. As the public school faculty took on different responsibilities, opportunities for dialogue increased and people communicated out of common experience.

Professors also moved into unfamiliar areas. Some of us took on the leadership of advisory groups and we experienced the same concerns, frustrations, and gratifications as teachers in the same role (see Trubowitz, 1994). Others entered classrooms to work with students as well as teachers. As college faculty moved into the role of teacher, their empathy for the practitioner has grown. One professor said: "I've learned a lot about how schools function, a lot about the life of teachers, a lot about special education, my own field. I've grown in my respect for people who work in schools. I appreciate more the complexity of schools and what administrators and teachers have to contend with."

When a principal becomes a professor, when a professor becomes a public school instructor, when a teacher becomes a college instructor or student teacher supervisor, when professors and public school teachers co-write articles or co-present at conferences, there develops a greater understanding of each other's role and the sense of separateness diminishes between institutions. However, preventing the traditional gap from reappearing requires continued attention and thought. It is more than the physical separation of the institutions that requires such preventative measures. There are differences of function, perspective, and tradition that need to be dealt with continually if the best that collaboration has to offer is achieved.

CHAPTER 7

A Broader View of
How Learning Occurs

MOVING BEYOND THE CLASSROOM

We came to the collaboration with the belief that learning should not be restricted to the confines of a single classroom within a single building. We further believed that experiences outside the classroom, outside the school, and beyond the normal school day and school year, introduce a different kind of reality and should be integrated into what goes on as part of curriculum exploration.

We wanted to create an atmosphere that would give free rein to the imagination and not demand teacher obeisance to a mandated curriculum. We looked forward to a school that saw community education as not only a way of providing learning opportunities for community residents, but also as a way of utilizing the many experiences and skills of neighborhood people. We sought to show that student interests and needs could be the basis for curriculum activity. Most of all, we sought ways to demonstrate our belief that these hopes could become reality.

Early Bird Program

Rare is the time in schools that shared enthusiasm becomes the fuel to energize curriculum exploration. The Early Bird program, as the 8:00 to 8:40 a.m. time before first period became called, illustrated a curriculum based on matching interests. The program was formed in recognition of the fact that most of what takes place in school severely restricts choice for both the learner and the teacher. In a compulsory educational setting, not only student attendance but most curriculum is mandated by forces outside the school. We sought an opportunity to bring students and teachers together around a curriculum of their own choosing. Teachers designed and described content offerings. Students reviewed the descriptions and decided whether they wanted to come to school forty minutes earlier and participate. (Approximately 250 students attended each morning.)

It is the only time in the school day when teachers and learners come together solely by choice and the program has proven quite successful. The topics are taught not only by teachers but by college interns and student teachers as well. Sample offerings have included chess, poetry workshops, sign language, storytelling, cooking classes, computer games, sand painting, guitar instruction, and, of course, topics in all the content areas. In groups of anywhere from 5 to 15, children voluntarily come together to pursue a topic of interest. The hope is that the enthusiasm of the teacher for the content will inspire learners to deeper exploration and continued interest in the topic.

In addition to the values inherent in the different subjects, the Early Bird program has had other benefits. Parents who are off to work early now feel easier about leaving their children at school where they can be involved in meaningful activity under supervision. The Early Bird program gives interns and student teachers a chance to work with small groups of children minimizing management problems for the novice teacher and allowing them to get to know middle schoolers in an informal environment. The value of informality and small group size is illustrated by the girl who responded to an adult's question about what she wanted to be when she grew up by saying, "I want to be a student teacher." When the adult tried to correct her by remarking, "You mean you want to be a teacher," the child replied, "No, I want to be a student teacher like my Early Bird teacher." The Early Bird program shows that interest can be a strong motivating force for curriculum exploration. When teachers and students are given choices and volunteer their participation, there will be a deeper investment of energy and effort than would ordinarily be expected.

The Early Bird program combined the practical value of giving work-bound parents a place to leave their children with the opportunity for novice professionals to practice their craft in a meaningful context.

Camp Armstrong

Two major concerns for entering middle school students are fear of the unknown and lack of familiarity with their new surroundings. The transition from the sheltered environment of the neighborhood elementary school to the less personal, more distant middle school arouses trepidation in new pupils and their parents. The unknown produces many such questions: "Will the other kids like me?" "Will my child be safe?" "Do the students carry guns?"

We have attempted to minimize these concerns by conducting a two-week orientation just prior to the opening of school. Entering students are invited to participate in a program that offers them a preview of what some of their classes and responsibilities will be like. The program is conducted in the morning, and students are given a modified schedule in which they are exposed to what the school schedule will be like. The schedule permits them to move through the school so they become familiar with the location of classrooms, special facilities (e.g., gym, shop, library), and services (administrative offices, counselors, nurses). Thus they have the chance to become familiar with the building, to meet some of their teachers, to play games in the gymnasium and the outside yard, to do hands-on science, and to enjoy a day's outing at the Queens College Environmental Center in Long Island. The first exposure of new students to the school is informal and combines fun with serious academic work. The students are exposed without the upper grades present, to what the school and their schedule will be like. They get the chance to make friends and, in general, learn to feel at ease in the school. The program serves to alleviate many of the fears students have about unfamiliar surroundings and what to expect *before* the actual school year begins.

Parents too worry about the new middle school experience. We bring them together during Camp Armstrong to discuss their concerns, to share views about effective ways to deal with preadolescents, and to give them information about the school's program. The inclusion of parents represents an awareness that, as students travel the path from childhood to adolescence, their parents experience their own journey into another stage of their role that will make considerable demands upon their patience and understanding. They also need opportunity to vent and share ideas about their changing circumstances. Camp Armstrong communicates the feeling that the total school community is welcoming newcomers, with teachers, administrators, college professors, seventh- and eighth-graders and their parents, all participating as guides and resource people.

The values of Camp Armstrong are substantiated by the teacher who said, "Having the kids early gives us a running start when school opens. The building isn't strange to them. They know us and we know them." Another teacher remarked, "The kids lose much of their fear—fear of other kids, fear of teachers, fear of the building."

The School-Community Museum

For most school children a trip to the museum means a long bus ride, a race past exhibits, a museum guide attempting to do justice to the works of masters in mere seconds, and a gobbled lunch in a noisy, crowded cafeteria. Pupils at the LAMS have a different view of a museum, because one has been created in their own school. Named after Al Oliver, the first superintendent-liaison from the Central Board of Education, the museum has become a center for many kinds of learning. An early exhibit comprised of etchings, cellotypes, and haiku poetry by children from Japan led pupils to write their own haiku poems and to experiment with printmaking techniques taught to them in workshops conducted in the museum. In addition, a music teacher taught Japanese songs and a home economics class prepared Japanese food.

The museum has continued to flourish and has frequently been used to facilitate the integration of subject matter. For example, a group of classes working with interns converted the museum into a replica of La Marqueta, the Puerto Rican market located at 116th Street and Park Avenue in New York City. The finished installation included paintings of the entrance to the market (complete with graffiti) and of the overhead railroad tracks. The students constructed pâpier maché copies of the various fruits, for example, mangoes and plantains. Stories were told in the museum about Hispanic customs and ideas. The music teacher taught the children songs and dances of Hispanic origin. Replicas of little shops were set up complete with price tags for items.

The museum has served to stimulate teachers to move into different curriculum areas. A recent exhibition of *arpilleras* (Peruvian wall hangings) motivated classes to investigate Peru and other South American countries. A group of nuns enriched class visits to the museum by telling stories of working with the Peruvian women who wove the *arpilleras*.

Each year, the museum hosts a faculty show, which, among other things, serves the purpose of helping the student see another side of their teachers. Surprise fills the faces of pupils as they view the artistic efforts of individuals they had no idea sculpted, painted, or knitted. The show reveals another dimension of the lives of many teachers that we feel has been highly beneficial in countering the one-dimensional view students often have of teachers.

The pupils at Louis Armstrong no longer see museums as distant, strange places to be visited infrequently and hurriedly. Instead, the museum has become a regular and familiar part of the school and its curriculum. It has become a place where children express themselves creatively both in art and language arts; where they experience art in its many forms (photography, painting, mobiles, and poetry); where they gain special satisfaction from seeing their work exhibited. The museum has become a location that reflects community life through exhibitions of the works of local artists and of the results of community studies. We would add here that the idea of a school museum has spread with Queens College graduates involved in programs at the Nassau County Museum of Fine Arts in Roslyn, at the Queens Museum in Flushing, and at the art museum located in Long Beach. Exhibitions launched at the Louis Armstrong Museum have traveled to other sites. Most recently, the simulation of the Puerto Rican market has been borrowed by the Museo del Barrio.

MOVING BEYOND THE SCHOOL INTO THE COMMUNITY

Education is a fluid enterprise not restricted to any one locale. In the collaboration we have sought to break down barriers between school and community. We believed that the world outside the classroom can provide strong motivation for learning. We also felt that it is a school's responsibility to be part of a learning society that responds to the needs of not only its children but also to the neighborhood's inhabitants.

People in the Community as a Resource

People in the community represent a rich resource for learning. This became clearly evidenced as teachers involved children in oral history projects. With the assistance of Arthur Tobier (1992), a college consultant with vast experience in chronicling stories of "artists and artisans, teachers and tradesmen, immigrants and emigres, neighborhood heroes and heroines" (p. 3), faculty have introduced another view of history, one that expresses the belief that in the experience of ordinary people in a community there is much to be learned about events of the past, present, and even the future.

The development of oral histories brings a reality to students' perception and understanding of historical events. It connects them to these events through family history. In a monograph written by a LAMS teacher and Queens College professor (Corvasce and Zarnowski, 1993), the words of a Korean child's immigrant father communicate so much more vividly the struggle of newcomers to our country than any textbook description:

> I came to America when I was 29 years old and already married. I had no relatives to help me, only a friend. The first night I slept in the YMCA because it was the cheapest place. The next day I moved in with my friend and shared his rooms. The next 2 or 3 years were the hardest. I had to adapt my lifestyle to America, which was very, very difficult. I had to learn the language very fast because I could not communicate. The way of thinking here is different from how I grew up. The cultural differences and the many things Americans do were funny to me. So many things I do American people didn't understand. I had to adjust to customs and culture fast. Even when I got a job, it was not easy for me to perform because of the communication problem. Now, 20 years later, I have pretty much adjusted. (p. 23)

Other important historical events come alive through the stories obtained from local inhabitants. The depression years gain an immediacy from the following:

> My grandfather was first aware of events outside of his house during the Depression, when his family had little food or money. Discussions about these problems were the first family conversations on events in the outside world. The Depression affected my grandfather profoundly. My first job was when I was 12, sweeping in a drug store. I made $2 a week. I ran home when I got paid and gave the money to my mother, who needed it desperately. A neighbor of ours managed a dress shop on 14th Street. He gave me a job on Saturdays, and paid me $3 for the day, to put dresses back on the rack and to take out boxes. I always remembered and appreciated what he did for me and my family. (p. 24)

In the course of interviewing parents, grandparents, and others, children do not only experience the relevance of history, they gain a connectedness to older residents of the community that might otherwise be missing.

Community History Day

Schools operate like space stations in the middle of a foreign environment, and most of all concerned with preventing outside contaminants from entering. Our perception of how schools should operate has been different. We have tried to recognize the richness of the community, its history and the contributions of its inhabitants. Most recently, the school, the college, and the Parent Teachers Association (PTA) sponsored a Community History Day, where people who had lived in the neighborhood 40, 50, or 60 years came together to relate stories of growing up and living in East Elmhurst, the community where the school is located. Florence Johnson, who lived in the area for 60 years, told about being the first black to integrate Flushing High School. Dr. George Lopez, a neighborhood dentist, described a time when no blacks were allowed to walk Ditmars Boulevard (a major community thoroughfare) and Mafia bigwigs lived in the mansions overlooking the bay. Others remembered Malcolm X speaking his views in local barber shops. A display of old photographs added to the trip back in time. The day's discussions supported the view that history is what happens to real people. We heard firsthand about the civil rights movement, immigration, industrial development, blockbusting, and human interaction.

The day was characterized by a warmth that emanates when people gather together to share reminiscences. The pride these long-time residents of the community felt was evident in such comments as: "I don't want to live any place else." "I didn't know I was poor." "People dressed with class." "We were called the Corona Debs." "Blacks and Whites lived together in peace and harmony."

The Community History celebration communicated the idea that the school cared about the community and its beginnings. The meeting represented the launching of a project to develop community archives to be housed in the school library.

Community Service

Middle School students need to know that they are needed, that their contributions count, and that adults value what they do. All too often schools deliver the message that students must act as responsible citizens, and yet they are given little opportunity to serve in responsible roles. Over the years LAMS has been involved in providing community service experience. During 1995, over 200 students, evenly divided between boys and girls, worked at a day-care center, a nursing home, and at a nearby elementary school. At the day-care center student helpers assist workers in play supervision, arts and crafts, nature walks, and diaper changing. The intergenerational program features arts and crafts, special parties, and roundtable discussions to consider issues of mutual interest to senior citizens and adolescents. In the elementary school, special education students read stories to younger children. These experiences take prior planning and involve time devoted to reflecting on what occurred. Preparation included lessons in child development, discussions of perceptions of the elderly, and rehearsing with one another stories to be read aloud to the younger children. Weekly sessions were held to share service experiences, develop problem solving and communication skills, and talk about possible careers. The comments of one student regarding her experience at the senior citizens center exemplify the reactions of others. She said, "I learned that even when you're old you've got spirit and excitement. I used to say, 'Oh, what can they do?' and I sure learned a lot. I'm even learning from my adopted grandfather's mistakes. I think this was the greatest experience I've had in school." If early adolescence is a developmental stage characterized by narcissism, service is one way to move beyond behavior that focuses on "me" and on to the satisfaction of exploring "we."

Community Mentorship

History and recent reports about education in other countries tell us that students working as apprentices under the guidance of adults in real-life situations provide invaluable learning. At LAMS the observations of participants in a voluntary after-school program give evidence of how serving with adults has helped them to learn about the world of work. One said, "In my work at the LaGuardia Airport main terminal, I learned that an airport is a kind of community; each person has a job to do. If they don't do it, it messes up everybody." Another reported, "I started out working just one afternoon a week at the TV and radio repair service. Now I work three afternoons after school and all day Saturday. One of the big things I learned was in answering the phone how to give a good impression. Of course, I found out a lot about how to fix TVs too." Another remarked, "I got to go with my mentor, Councilman Joe Lisa, to a city council meeting. It was fascinating! Holly and Tracy, who work with state senator Ivan Lafayette and councilwoman Helen Marshall, made special trips too. They went all the way to Albany to see the state legislature in action." In the collaboration we sought constantly to move curriculum beyond the traditional boundaries of textbooks and tests. We wanted to take advantage of reality, to give children a chance to learn about government, jobs, people, themselves, all in the context of actual work experience.

Parents as Part of the School Community

We believed that the family represents the primary teaching environment and that parental encouragement, support, supervision, and positive communication about school and learning are a powerful influence on student achievement, grades, attitudes, aspiration, and behavior. We sought ways to enable more parents to become involved in their children's education. We faced large challenges to our efforts to include parents in the life of the school. They included the following:

- Counter the myth that early adolescents are so focused on the importance of peer relationships and the drive to establish a sense of independence that they no longer want or need parental attention.
- Alleviate the sense of inadequacy some parents feel about dealing with their children as they approach the full bloom of adolescence.
- Deal with parental lack of knowledge of subject matter areas with which they are unfamiliar.
- Overcome the fact that students come from all over the borough of Queens, and that geographical distance hinders the development of a cohesive parent group.
- Work with a changing family unit with families headed by a single parent or mother and father both working.
- Interact with a parent group representing diverse cultures with different attitudes towards the school as an institution.

- Define appropriate roles for parents, as new concepts of shared school management are introduced.

We began by providing information at the open house meetings to recruit pupils to the school and at the summer orientation sessions conducted during Camp Armstrong. Information was given regarding school programs, personnel, and policies. During the summer orientation meeting, time has always been reserved to conduct a workshop for helping parents on how to deal with the emerging adolescent. For many years these meetings were led by college personnel. Recently, leadership for these sessions has moved to the parents themselves, some of whom have taken special training in parent education. These parent-led efforts have been conducted throughout the year with information shared about health and safety, nutrition, discipline and guidance, parenting skills, and parenting approaches. This information is disseminated not only at workshops but also through newsletters, at parent conferences, and through handouts.

We have found that the key to effective interactions between groups — whether between college personnel and teachers or college staff and parents — is that even though professors come with a certain expertise, they also come as learners. There needs to be a recognition that no one constituency possesses all the insight or has the best understanding of every experience. For example, just as schools can assist families to understand child and adolescent development, families can help schools to understand family life and students' needs, interests, and talents.

An instance of learning for one of the authors occurred when he was leading a discussion with a group of parents about effective ways of working with young adolescents. At one point he was stressing the value of touching as a way of showing affection when a Hindu parent interjected the thought that in his culture adults did not use physical contact to express closeness with children. He realized that what had been accepted as a truism was not always the case, for other cultures espouse different child-rearing approaches. It was not his role to disagree but rather to listen, learn, and show respect for another perspective about how parents relate to their children.

We looked for ways to involve parents in the life of the school. For years we hosted meetings where, early in the school term, parents joined with teachers and college staff at an all-day meeting held at the Queens College Center to discuss goals for the year. At the end of the year, another similar session took place to evaluate progress toward achievement of goals.

Another opportunity for parent participation is the school-based management team, which provides another place for parents to express their views. Discussions have been enriched by ideas coming from their vantage point. For example, it was the parents who brought into focus the inadequacies of the belt-line system of parent–teacher conferencing that allowed less than five minutes for discussion of a child's progress. It was the parents who expanded the purpose of the conference to include the idea of teachers learning about children from parents, as well as teachers reporting on a child's progress. As they worked on committees devoted to such topics as nutrition, school environment, bus safety, and curriculum, parents became more integrated into the life of the school and less the outside viewers who needed to be impressed and kept ignorant of school problems. Parent comments point to the value of their participation: "Serving on the school-based management team gives you a sense of the heartbeat of the school." "It is the most candid relationship that one can experience in the school." "I've learned ways to help my child better." "Teachers have begun to look to parents as sources of information."

In the collaboration we have recognized that family life affects school life. With the assistance of a college guidance intern, a guidance school counselor established a divorce group made up of children whose parents had split. These students, all of whom participated with parent permission, discussed their feelings about home events. They talked about parents arguing and blaming each other, their responses to parents' problems, and how they could best deal with particular situations. Another benefit resulted from the school–college collaboration when the Queens College Marriage and Family Counseling Program established LAMS as a place for their interns to work with families, with supervision to be provided by the school's guidance counselors — all of whom were graduates of the Queens program. In this way a resource was added to the school and the college had found a site to give interns practical experience under careful supervision.

Relationships develop over time as people have opportunities to do things together. For it is the communication that occurs in informal situations that is most effective. When parents accompany teachers on trips, attend the school–college retreats, or meet at the annual parent–teacher dinner dance, "education talk" occurs under more natural circumstances.

The School as Part of the Community

We wanted a community school that would serve adults as well as children. From the start classes were held to teach English to newcomers to the country. Senior citizens came to the school for classes in literature, politics, and music. College professors gave lectures at the museum on

Soviet education and African art. Adults walking through the halls of LAMS are a common sight. As adults have had the chance to see the school more closely, as they participate in the decision-making affecting their children, and as they observe teachers and students reaching out to utilize the rich resources of the community, the LAMS has become a valued neighborhood institution. The colorful mural of Louis Armstrong and his friends that is at the entrance of the school has become the school's signature and symbolizes the community's acceptance of the school. The mural, painted the year of the school's opening with the assistance of teenagers from Elmcor (a local community agency), Louis Armstrong pupils, and Queens College students, and taking up a large amount of space, is a tempting target for graffiti artists. Over the years the mural has remained virtually untouched, testimony to the neighborhood's acceptance of the school. The gleeful faces of Louis and his friends continue to peer down at visitors to the school with unmarred faces.

MAINTAINING AN INTEGRATED SCHOOL

The task of maintaining an integrated school in New York City has increased in difficulty as more and more whites have fled to the suburbs to avoid urban problems. For 17 years despite the diminishing pool of Whites in the borough of Queens, the collaboration has succeeded in meeting the requirements of the court order calling for a student population that is 55 percent minority and 45 percent nonminority. The fact that each year the school receives over 3000 applications allows the recruitment of sufficient numbers of minority and nonminority children. (We would point out here that in a recent survey of parents asking them to indicate the factors that drew them to apply to the school, 80% indicated the college's involvement as a major reason.)

The effort to maintain an integrated school has been supported by the college's insistence that classes be organized on a heterogeneous basis. We wanted to demonstrate that it was possible to deal effectively with children who not only represent racial and ethnic differences, but who also were selected on the basis of academic diversity with 25% of the students below grade level, 50% on grade, and 25% above. Our experience told us that schools which had classes divided into top and bottom groups (sometimes less kindly referred to as the "smart" and the "dumb") found teachers vying for the top classes and the slow classes becoming centers of hostility and disruption. Research substantiated our point of view, for it showed that throughout the grades, race, social class, and track assignment correlate consistently with low-income students and non-Asian minorities disproportionately enrolled in low-track academic classes, and advantaged students and Whites more often enrolled in the high track.

Our success in making heterogeneity an integral part of the school design was not easily achieved. In discussions prior to the opening of the school, when college faculty introduced the concept of heterogeneous organization, it was clear that Board of Education representatives had serious reservations about abandoning an approach that was widespread throughout the city. It was only because the college's affiliation was needed that they agreed to go along.

The support for heterogeneity has resulted in classes comprised of children of different races and backgrounds. Some students have had their first ongoing experience of working in an interracial group. The heterogeneous class has also impelled teachers to consider ways of working with children of varying abilities. Teachers have introduced cooperative learning, integrated curriculum areas, arranged for more hands-on experiences, and collaborated more closely with their colleagues. Just as teachers' exposure to different kinds of children has increased, students have had greater contact with different quality teachers. The presence of bright students in every class made for parental pressure, urging teachers to make certain that their children's abilities are challenged.

We were not so naive as to believe that the alternative to rigid homogeneity was simply to stop tracking. We realized that in the complex social, educational, and political context of the school, problems would arise as we attempted to establish classes made up of children of varying ability. For example, bureaucratic rigidity has been an obstacle, as the State Department of Education has mandated accelerated classes for eighth-graders in mathematics and science. This has functionally served to encourage homogeneous grouping of the eighth-graders in these areas. The school itself continues to have features that inhibit detracking. They include a reporting system based on numerical grades derived from uniform assessment procedures, lack of teacher skill in differentiating curriculum, parental pressure to make special accommodation for the intellectually gifted, a range of curriculum offerings focusing primarily on verbal talent, a departmentalized structure for the upper grades, and an absence of commitment on the part of some teachers to the concept of heterogeneity. This latter group remains firm in its belief that education is competitive and distinctions between individuals and groups need to be made.

From the beginning the problems have been addressed. College consultants have worked with teachers to help them modify curriculum and to become familiar with a cooperative learning approach. Opportunities for those with special talents have been made available through the Early Bird program, Saturday classes, and special summer projects. (For example, through a project at another college, youngsters with particular capability in science have had a chance to participate in a summer instructional program.)

Despite these problems, for the most part classes are heterogeneously grouped and LAMS has avoided a situation where the school is outwardly integrated but inwardly segregated. Thus far, we have managed to have children play, work, and learn together despite difference of race, ethnicity, or ability.

Developing Respect for All Cultures

Another factor contributing to the maintenance of an integrated pupil population has been an emphasis on making the diversity of student backgrounds a source of curriculum exploration.

One of the authors has remarked, not with total seriousness but with some justification, that if the school were to do little else than have the children talk about their own families, backgrounds, customs, food, language, and holidays, a rich curriculum would result. In fact, it has become common practice for teachers of the fifth and sixth grades to begin the school year with what has been called the "You" curriculum. Children in these classes construct family trees, interview parents, bring artifacts from home, teach each other dances and songs, and create time lines of family history.

As noted earlier in this chapter, museum exhibitions have fostered appreciation of other cultures. The recent showing of *arpilleras* stimulated interest in South America while "El Mercado," the museum simulation of a Puerto Rican market, demonstrated how important it is for immigrant populations to recreate a sense of place when they move to a new country. Students visiting the museum for that exhibit learned directly about the foods, the music, the clothing, and the language of Puerto Rico as they journeyed through island life. In a similar vein, other cultures have been highlighted through exhibitions of the work of African-American photographers, the artwork of Russian children, and the poetry of Japanese youngsters.

People with ideas for special projects have found a welcome reception at LAMS. Among these projects have been those with a focus on intergroup relations. One such project is Facing History, a program designed to educate children about racism through a study of the Holocaust. African-American, Asian-American, White, Muslim, Christian, Hindu, and Jewish children are exposed to stories, films, class discussions, and to actual Holocaust survivors, so they become familiar with the horrors of racism carried to the extreme. They are helped to see parallels in other countries at other times—in Armenia, in the former Yugoslavia, in the days of American slavery. They confront such questions as:

- What responsibility do we have for one another as neighbors and as nations?
- How can people and groups confront racism?
- What causes apathy and how can we overcome it?
- What issues do we need to explore in order to create a more humane society?

In a school made up of children of different backgrounds and races, a project that attempts to cultivate understanding and empathy for others has special significance. By reflecting on their own experiences with racism and looking at the lives of others who have been victims of discrimination, children begin to see more clearly their own role as part of a world community. We believe they develop a greater respect and appreciation for differences and see the similarities among groups and people. It helps them begin to look at things as they really are which, as one child stated, "is a form of growing up."

Exploration of the Holocaust, and most likely of any aspect of intergroup relations, is not without complications—a fact which emphasizes the need for the subject's study. In this era of religious and racial conflict there will be those who say, "Why are we spending so much time learning about the plight of the Jews?" They may fail to see the connection between what occurred during the Holocaust and what has happened and could happen to others. Our goal is the building of a sense of community that understands what happens to one has implications for all.

Project Equal

Another example of a project designed to help middle school children to better understand their own experience and to empathize with children from different backgrounds is Project Equal. Its aim has been to help teachers, librarians, and students to appreciate differences and to recognize universals. The project bases its curriculum on the reading of trade books specially selected for their presentation of different cultures. Discussions center around the concept of stereotyping and the consequences of prejudice and discrimination. A fifth-grade student gave her description of the program: "Project Equal is a program to educate children about prejudices and stereotyping. We read and discuss books in groups about kids that face problems. Project Equal teaches us how to handle tough situations. Hopefully we'll make the right decisions. Sometimes our friends are doing something that is wrong but we can't go along with the crowd. We have to stand up and stick to what we believe in. Project Equal taught us about life, values, courage, and most importantly, human respect" (quoted in Johnson & Smith, 1993, p. 1).

These efforts to promote equality are not without problems. Project Equal has provided us with yet another instance illustrating the fallacy of the belief that simply to introduce a program will result in the achievement of the desired goal. One example occurred with the use of the book *Friends* by Rosa Guy. A well-written book of quality, it became a source of concern for some teachers because it presented a teacher in a bad light and showed children reacting to her cruel, insensitive behavior with racial and religious epithets. The dispute became heated as a teacher said, "Why should you encourage children to read a book that shows teachers as bigots, as cruel human beings?" Others defended the use of the book and decried the effort to keep the book from children as censorship. Emotions were inflamed and representatives of the Board of Education's Bureau of Libraries were summoned to present a defense for the book. People chose sides and barricaded themselves behind intransigent beliefs.

It was here that the view of the college as an objective participant in school activity proved useful: We were able to arrange a meeting where differences between those who advocated use of the book and those who felt offended by some of its content were aired, for the solution to the problem lay in the opportunity for reasoned dialogue. One result was the understanding that realistic fiction may introduce negative stereotypes but that this material can become a rich source for sensitive, in-depth discussion. Another was that those who felt offended by the stereotypes have a right to have their feelings expressed and respected. It highlights the potential for problems, even when the best of intentions are present and the valuable role that collaborators can play if they demonstrate a reasonable degree of objectivity. It also illustrates the fact that the introduction of a new program may initially exacerbate problems they were originally intended to solve.

Our success in keeping classes heterogeneously organized and highlighting the different cultures represented in the school has contributed to the maintenance of LAMS as an integrated school. But, finally, it is the ability to create what is seen as a "good" school, one in which there is a safe supportive environment, a variety of exciting programs, meaningful curriculum, opportunity for success for all children, and a caring staff that has resulted in the large numbers of parents of all races and backgrounds who each year apply for admission to the school.

Our attempts to move LAMS beyond the classroom and outside the boundaries of the school day and school year were meant to implement the view that education should not solely be based on books and not restricted to a single place. We have sought to build connections with other people and other locations. We wanted to use the diversity of interests and backgrounds represented in the school as a means of strengthening our students' understanding of themselves and others.

LEARNING OUTCOMES

We hasten to note that this broader view of what constitutes important outcomes for learning has not been maintained at the expense of traditional academic performance. Students at LAMS have done exceptionally well on all objective measures of academic progress over the years. Standardized test results have constantly placed the school in the top 10% of middle schools in New York City, a trend that has remained consistent over the 17 years the school has been in existence.

Additionally, some 75% of our graduates go on to specialized or screened high schools, where entrance is competitive and available seats limited. In the same way that they or their parents chose to attend LAMS, these students have investigated and then successfully pursued their choice for a high school setting compatible with their interests or abilities. We believe that both the determination displayed in this process and the documented academic ability that allows the desired outcome to be achieved reflect credit on the school and its students.

CHAPTER 8

Preservice Teacher Training: The Internship

Reforms worthy of the name are always slow; and reform even of governments and churches is not so slow as that of schools, for there is the great preliminary difficulty of fashioning the instruments — of teaching the teachers.

— *John Stuart Mill, quoted in Garfarth, 1971*

From the beginning of the collaboration, the college staff sought ways to make connections between its mission to prepare teachers and the goal of making LAMS an outstanding middle school. Preservice teachers at various levels of training — observers, participants, student teachers — were placed in the school. Because the college assumed responsibility for creating, organizing, and curating the museum space in the school, several graduate students pursuing degrees in art education were added to the undergraduate group of preservice trainees assigned to the school.

In a short time, graduate students preparing to teach in a wide variety of content areas were invited to participate, and a specialized internship program was created. Interns were assigned to work at the school three full days a week in exchange for a modest stipend and free tuition for the bulk of their graduate program.

WHO ARE OUR INTERNS?

From its very inception, the internship program took on a special character. To begin with, we were dealing with graduate students, many of whom had not majored in education as undergraduates. For these students, teaching was a change of career choice. The vast majority had spent several years in other occupations before deciding upon teaching. Such individuals brought to the program a mature outlook, a rich background of experience, good academic preparation, and a high level of motivation. Since only 12 to 15 interns a year were chosen, the college staff was able to fill these positions from a sizable pool of applicants. Whether it was due

120

to the competition for available slots, the breadth of prior experience, or the simple self-selection resulting from the kind of risk-taking such career change requires, the program was able to attract individuals with a high level of ability.

Over the past 15 years, the College staff has continued to shape and refine the overall framework of the internship. Regarding its use as a vehicle for teacher training, it shares much in common with other internship programs across the nation. The particular approach that has evolved, however, focuses on several key features that we believe are vitally important and, when taken together, make the approach we use somewhat different from many of the currently available models.

First, we believe that interns should not be employees of the school system they are serving and, most importantly, should not be assigned their own class. Our experience indicates that if the interns are to really test their skills, take risks, and find out what works best for them, it is vital that they not have final responsibility for the class. Internship models that make new teachers fully accountable for a class while offering a reduced day for training generally place interns in a position where the requirements of the job generate a set of demands that overwhelm the time provided for reflection. There is then little energy and often less inclination for interns so burdened to complicate their professional lives any further by experimenting with new curriculum and teaching approaches, or reflecting at any great length on the meaning of their role.

Reflective Learning

The activity of reflection has almost always been a by-product of leisure time and reduced responsibility. Full-time work is more likely to produce pragmatists, people intent on preparing for the moment and insuring that the responsibility assigned is performed according to standard expectations. There are exceptions, but one would assume that those assigned a task in need of their immediate attention are more likely to seize upon and use the tools and techniques that are readily available. For teaching, these include former and present role models as well as materials and approaches that are generally in use. An internship built on such a model is likely to produce many teachers who reflect the norm for classroom instruction, but few who exceed it.

The day-to-day demands of classroom responsibility tend to direct the efforts of new teachers away from experimentation and reflection and toward techniques that will simply reproduce standard practice. This kind of approach to an internship is useful because it offers new teachers the support they need, but it does not offer the profession trainees who have had adequate opportunity to explore new horizons and find their own teaching voice.

A School-wide Experience

A second feature of the internship revolves around our belief that interns should be assigned to a school and not a classroom. We have consciously decided *not* to emulate the standard student teaching model. In that approach, trainees are assigned to a classroom where they work closely with a single teacher over an extended period of time. We wanted to expose interns to a broad variety of teaching styles and approaches. Only in this way could real comparisons be made regarding classroom management techniques, means of establishing rapport with students, and the varied instructional strategies that veteran teachers employ.

If trainees are to be encouraged to experiment and test what approaches work best for them, they must be exposed to a variety of styles among which they can choose. Most importantly, opportunities must be provided that allow trainees to employ the chosen approach in an environment that is hospitable to it. Testing an instructional strategy that is predicated on student freedom in a classroom that has been tightly managed is an invitation to disaster. Too often it is the strategy, not its misguided application, that is blamed and abandoned by the novice. To persist in trying alternative ways of organizing a classroom or conducting an instructional program, one must be exposed to successful models. That is far more likely to happen if the school — and not a single classroom — is the venue for the intern's efforts.

Classroom Observation

Interns in our program spend the first month of the school year observing as many classrooms as they can. They are asked not to confine themselves to a single grade level or their own content area, but to observe widely and use the opportunity to reflect on different aspects of the classroom. Over time we ask them to shift their focus — from the teacher, to the student, to the mechanics of the classroom environment. Within each of these areas further observational subtopics are focused upon, such as teacher-questioning techniques, student assignments, or the use of classroom space.

The intent of this full observation schedule is twofold: to expose the interns to a broad variety of teaching styles and to prepare them to make choices about the classrooms where they feel they have useful contributions to make. Interns are then free to approach teachers with suggestions for units of study they can teach within the observed framework. Over the next several weeks their schedules will reflect a program of continued observation combined with teaching. As the semester progresses, it will be possible to find interns working at several grade levels with different teachers conducting five- or six-week units of study. Over the year, it is common to have deeper and continuing attachments to one or two classrooms, but observation and activity with other classes continue.

It must be noted that many years of collaborative activity in the school have given the program access to most classrooms. There remain teachers who are uncomfortable being observed, particularly at the beginning of the year when they are building rapport with their students. While this is precisely what we want our interns to observe, it is a given that we do not press such individuals for entry to their classrooms. This response is in part a measure of the respect and high regard we hold for the work of the teachers, a respect that compels us to recognize how delicate the balance is in the classroom. It is also a recognition of one of the unwritten rules of the teaching culture — professionals are typically not free to observe one another. Observation of instruction is a prerogative confined to supervisory personnel. Perhaps it is a tradition that has evolved in recognition of the fact that teaching involves making oneself vulnerable before others. There are no guarantees that on a particular day even tried and true approaches will not fall flat, leaving the teacher with a deep sense of frustration or failure. Few will choose to invite spectators when such a prospect is in the offing.

The existence of such an unwritten code is one of the reasons we have made observation such a key aspect of the internship. We note for interns that unless things change, it is unlikely they will ever again have the chance to conduct such widespread observation of other professionals — unless they become supervisors. Such opportunity is likely to be confined to their current status and the unique acceptance the program has won from teachers.

Enhanced Supervisory Guidance

A fourth key aspect of the internship is the enhanced supervisory guidance that is provided. The college staff attached to the project believed that the supervision of novices had to be more extensive. Our experience with the student teaching model, where the supervisor made several site visits during the course of the semester to observe, convinced us that such an approach provided insufficient support to sustain any real innovative or exploratory efforts. As a result, the decision was made to provide a supervisor on-site during the days interns were working at the school. The presence of such an on-site supervisor has had a number of distinct advantages. Over time, personnel in that position have been able to develop closer working relationships with teachers in the school. This has enabled us to make more informed suggestions to interns about where they can observe and for what particular purposes. In a similar vein, we have been able to provide more effective guidance regarding teaching, encouraging better matches between the abilities and interests of the interns and available classroom environments. This more detailed knowledge of the school environment has also allowed us to suggest placements interns might seek when they are ready to extend certain skills or need support for new techniques or approaches.

As the years have passed, the on-site supervisor in the program has become a constant in the school while personnel in the trainee role remain the variable and change yearly. Such an arrangement is not always true of the student-teaching model, where college supervisors are frequently reassigned and a thorough knowledge of the school is not always viewed as a matter of great consequence. We have found that an ongoing, informed understanding of staff strengths and weaknesses has proven an invaluable aid in helping to sharpen and shape the skills of trainees.

An additional advantage of on-site supervision emerges in the conduct of weekly seminars with the interns. Again, such seminars are a common feature of practice teaching models. What the presence of an on-site supervisor has provided, however, is someone who can bring to the discussion an intimate understanding of the culture of this specific school, as well as a knowledge of particular teachers and the nature of the classroom environments in which the interns are working. A grasp of these important details can enrich the content of seminar discussions by providing useful background information and deflecting surface or stereotypical conclusions about classroom practices that interns have observed. Further, it can serve as a corrective to the "we–them" mentality that sometimes arises among trainees.

An essential aspect of the internship has been the attempt to wed theory and practice. This is perhaps the most consistent criticism made of teacher training programs. In our view, it is not an unwarranted criticism. The traditional nature of the school and college as educational institutions has resulted in theoretical aspects taught at the latter, with practice conducted under the auspices of the former. For reasons more fully developed later, we have not made as thorough an integration of the theory and practice as we would like. For the most part, practice still occurs in the public school while the theoretical or more abstract matters are discussed in a college setting far removed from the school site. Such distance can have its advantages. One tends to be less caught up in the personal and particular, and this can allow broader reflection about the general nature of school bureaucracy and what it allows or discourages in the way of educational practice. However, in practical terms most trainees find the emphasis in college classroom too removed from their concerns as teachers and, for the most part, less helpful than they want.

The seminar has represented one effort to bridge the gap. It is officially a college course, but it is conducted on site and taught by the intern supervisor. The course content includes numerous readings carefully chosen to provide both scholarly insight into problems and responses to issues interns have raised in their journals or during more informal discussions (e.g., brown bag lunches) at the school.

The remainder of the courses interns take are conducted at the college and because there is not a core of courses common to the different majors represented, they are not taken jointly. This has obvious drawbacks. What remains helpful is that the graduate study and the experience in the schools are happening at the same time. Interns are in the school during the day and take courses in the late afternoon or evening. The fact that the experiences are parallel, combined with the emphasis provided by the seminar, does afford interns reasonable opportunities to integrate theory and practice.

Creating a Peer Support System

A final feature of the program is the creation of a support system for participants. The purpose in developing such a system of support is to provide interns with the encouragement they need in the present and to offer them a skill they can employ in the future against the prospect of professional isolation. The intern supervisor is clearly a vital part of that support system. So are the college staff and consultants working on different projects in the school. Over the course of time interns are introduced to all and are offered the opportunity to observe or work with them on specific aspects of their endeavor. What has proven most helpful, however, has been the conscious, programmatic effort to form the interns into a support group for one another. From the ice-breaking activities conducted at the initial orientation session to their final day in the school, they are encouraged to work cooperatively and see themselves as a peer support system. The emphasis takes on a variety of forms. They are invited to share observations, conduct mutual research, and videotape each other teaching lessons. They are encouraged to team-teach, organize museum exhibits together, and work jointly on curriculum projects or unit development.

We have found such peer support to be invaluable. It serves a unique purpose that, in our experience, cannot be filled by either school staff or college faculty. Each has a distinctive role in meeting a particular set of needs, but we have found that good peer support has a special place. It encourages risk-taking and promotes more extensive efforts to capitalize upon opportunities for personal and professional development. It can be an effective part of the teacher-training process. It also has implications for future growth.

In emphasizing peer support we believe it is most important that interns are afforded the opportunity to break with what has been a persistent stereotype in education: that all teaching is conducted by one individual in isolation from professional colleagues. The vision of education we have encouraged has room in it to see teaching as a community enterprise. Most instruction in schools is restricted by an informal code of operation that completely isolates teachers and teaching. This leads to a tendency on the part of many teachers to similarly isolate learners and learning. Such a view is unnecessarily limiting and confining; it ignores the fact that teaching and learning are most often a communal process, a group activity that draws on a broad array of skills possessed by both teachers and learners. The creation of rigid boundaries both between and among the teaching and learning communities represents a prodigal misuse of the total pool of talent available. It is a configuration that often serves to make teaching a lonely and professionally isolating enterprise. The field has recently placed great emphasis on cooperative learning among students while continuing to ignore the value of similar cooperation among teachers. Attempts must be made to access the potential of combined efforts, for they can enhance the environment where schooling takes place. Emphasizing the value of peer support and cooperation is one useful step in that direction.

Teacher Recruitment

Apart from its value in training teachers, the usefulness of the internship as a teacher recruitment vehicle should also be mentioned. On average, about 20% of the LAMS staff is composed of former Queens College trainees. What the program provides is an opportunity for the school and the trainee to study one another with the prospect of future employment in mind. The school has suggested to us the instructional areas where there may be future need. Interns are recruited in such areas, and when there has been both an opening and an intern who has demonstrated the ability to fill it successfully, positions have been offered.

The advantages to the school are obvious. The program does the initial screening of candidates and affords school administration ample opportunity to directly observe the prospective teacher perform over time. The advantage for interns who accept such positions is that they have a good understanding of the school setting where they will work, know a large number of their future colleagues, and have a better feel for what they can expect from students and the administration.

There is also the related potential for school restructuring. College staff are currently contacting other urban middle schools, particularly those with high rates of teacher turnover. We hope to have interns hired in clusters of four or five, where they could continue to function as small support groups working closely together and sustaining one another's efforts. In our view this is the next logical extension of our program, and could help interns maintain their teaching vision while also providing schools with small pockets of innovative practice that could be built on to revitalize instructional efforts. It would also help if a structure could be created that would maintain a continuing relationship between newly employed interns and members of the college staff formerly involved in their training. If the mentoring of new teachers that New York State has — until recently — required could be employed for this purpose, it would be an excellent way of providing the kind of help needed by new teachers.

WHEN SCHOOL AND COLLEGE CONFLICT

Effective teacher training should concern itself not only with preparing novices to work in schools organized in traditional ways, but also with exposing them to alternatives, preparing them for possible changes that may occur. In order to accomplish this, the schools and the colleges must learn to work much more closely together. The divided responsibility for teacher training — for example, the model that has students taking courses at the college for one period and then practice teaching in the schools for another — results in two separate experiences that do not always complement one another. Many trainees complain of a dissonance that borders on schizophrenia. Too often what has resulted is that students, given one set of perspectives by the college, have those views challenged or totally contradicted by personnel in the schools. It is hardly a seamless garment, and the trainee is left with the awesome responsibility of trying to patch together an educational philosophy out of what seems like conflicting points of view about teaching and learning.

Obviously not all such conflict is bad. Different perspectives can sharpen understanding about one's beliefs. Still, it seems necessary to provide people new to the profession with some reasonable unity of purpose, particularly at a time when they are so vulnerable and in need of clear understanding to perform their tasks well. It is unfair, perhaps irresponsible, to continue a pattern of training where such conflicting messages are being sent.

In our view, the internship remains incomplete in this regard. The graduate courses remain an isolated part of the interns' training, one that is not consciously integrated with their day to day teaching experience. Such integration remains our ultimate challenge. The hope is that a core of courses can be developed (philosophy of education, learning theory, curriculum development, general methods of teaching) that would mutually satisfy requirements for the disparate majors (elementary education, special education, mathematics, science, art, history, English) represented in the program. These courses would be held on site and, like the seminar, would make use of the immediate environment to illuminate the curriculum and provide opportunities to directly test, review, and revise processes or perspectives that might otherwise be viewed as quaint theories. We have enjoyed little success thus far in attaining this goal, though some small progress has been made. Taking steps to unite the theoretical and practical, to allow each to challenge and inform the other, remains an urgent consideration for any of us involved in teacher training.

For too long the expectation has been that we can produce educational reform by making changes in either the way teachers are trained or the way our schools are run. The vast majority of effort has focused on the latter. Thus, there have been calls to either reorganize the schools or revise teacher training practices. It seems increasingly clear that little of real substance is going to happen until we find ways to combine these efforts and make simultaneous change in both institutions a priority. The internship promoted by this collaborative venture represents one such effort, and in this regard it has met with considerable frustration. As far as the college is concerned, the program remains a separate entity, an individual enterprise conducted by members of the staff in a different setting with goals that are viewed as interesting — but not central to the mission of the School of Education.

There is no one to blame in all this. The project is neither disparaged nor is it the recipient of negative criticism or blocking behavior. The internship simply remains an isolated phenomenon, and its implications for teacher training ignored. The resistance that appears seems the result of an inertia born of an underlying belief that a long-standing and perfectly useful program for training teachers is already in place. Why tinker with its essentials or seek to replace it? As with most resistance to change, that view is seen as not only pragmatically correct, but reasonable. Individuals and institutions in denial share at least one thing in common: No action will be undertaken about problems that are not believed to exist.

The difficulty is compounded by the fact that faculty from the college see themselves as essentially open to change — indeed, as change agents. There exists within this community a long-standing view that most of the impetus for change comes from the college, while most of the resistance to it comes from the schools. This is a comforting, if distorted, view of the way things are. From our experience the College has its own deep pockets of resistance. Staff can be very liberal about the organization or governance of other institutions, while remaining extremely conservative about their own. Change is made far more difficult when you do not see yourself as resistant to it. Perhaps it is that each institution has difficulty seeing or admitting to the changes that need to be made. It has long been evident to those in the schools, for example, that the colleges need to engage in some major rethinking about the way we train teachers.

None of this should be construed to mean that the public school as an institution does not present similar, deepseated opposition to change. Those of us working in the project are reminded daily that good intentions are not enough to bring about change in what is a complex organization deeply rooted in its own highly developed cultural environment. We are not seeking anything as ambitious as an overhaul of either or both institutions. What the collaborative has attempted is to unite staff from the two institutions in an effort to promote measured reforms in practices and processes that impinge on both.

Good organizations should seek ways to make the kind of changes that will prevent their becoming operationally dysfunctional. Lacking a well-organized research and development arm, the field of education can profit from many small efforts like ours that seek and suggest new directions that might be usefully pursued. The more difficult challenge is finding ways for such projects to get what they have learned adopted before the program itself disappears.

SUMMARY

We believe the internship has proven to be an exceptionally effective way of inducting trainees into the profession. It offers them a broader vision of education through exposure to a wide variety of teaching styles, emphasizes the need to understand the way the larger school setting influences instruction, and provides a support system comprised of individuals with varying levels of skill and/or experience. Because they have such support and work in a larger number of different settings, greater risk-taking and exploration of alternatives can be encouraged. Failure in one setting can be modified or corrected through efforts made elsewhere, with perhaps a different teacher, another grade level, or a class whose student chemistry is simply different or more receptive. Such expanded choice is not a mere palliative. It takes advantage of a rare opportunity to imbue trainees with a wider perspective about both what is happening in education and what may be possible.

As a training vehicle, the internship appears to have provided advantages for two distinct categories of graduate students. First were those trainees involved in change of career decisions who had no prior teaching experience and little previous training in education. The project has clearly served them well by building on their past experience and offering them teaching opportunities that give meaning to their program of study. We also serve a population of graduate students who have completed an undergraduate program in education and have student-taught; in this category those who have benefited the most are individuals who, for one reason or another, needed an extended practice teaching experience. Some had been in difficult student-teaching placements or simply did not have adequate opportunity to gain sufficient skill or confidence to take over their own classroom. Whatever the need, there is little question that the program has provided the additional time and opportunity some have needed to remain in the profession.

In closing, reference should be made to the next step we are taking to solidify the internship. We have recruited a dozen teachers in the school whose experience ranges from 2 to 10 years, and formed them into a teacher support group. In part, this is meant to provide an extended support system for interns. The two groups will meet regularly during the year to share reflections from their different vantage points about key issues facing classroom practitioners and to give interns the benefit of the teachers' experience. Beyond this, however, the meetings will also provide the veteran teachers with their own support system and a forum for discussing ideas and reflecting about their experience as professionals. Such opportunity for reflection seems much needed, yet it is rarely provided within the context of the regular school organization. We believe that if even experienced teachers are expected to grow, and most growth involves taking risks, they will need the support of colleagues who are similarly engaged. To see such commitment modeled should prove useful to trainees, but vital to experienced classroom teachers who are provided too few outlets for their own professional development.

PART IV

THE COLLABORATION
A Broader Overview

CHAPTER 9

Reflections on Collaboration

WORKING IN THE SCHOOLS

For those college staff who can make the necessary adjustments, working in the schools can be not only highly rewarding, but also the source of great professional stimulation. The capacity to profit from such participation is less a case of skill and experience than one of temperament and intent. It is not that experience does not help nor that considerable skill is not necessary, but that one must be willing to suspend judgment and admit to the great complexity of the enterprise in which one is engaged in order to fully profit from it. If you can come armed with a deep sense of purpose and yet remain open to the likelihood that you do not have all the answers, schools can be places of endless fascination. So much that is vital and truly important can happen there, that the work is worthy of the best that the most able among us have to offer.

This does not mean that tasks are easy or a source of continuous pleasure. For those who find activities which pose the least amount of threat to be the most rewarding, schools are the wrong venue. What has attracted us to the task is the demands it makes on your ability, imagination, and desire to shape a better future. The demands can often outstrip your capacity—a source of discouragement but also a spur to greater effort. The degree of satisfaction has often proven directly proportional to the complexity of the challenge presented.

We have frequently asked ourselves why we have chosen to spend such a significant portion of our time in the schools rather than remaining full time at the college. The best answer we can give is that for us, the dual role has simply proven more satisfying. Lest we be accused of "school chauvinism" or similar crimes, let us hasten to add that this view is a personal one and not intended as prescriptive for others. As we noted earlier, most of the boundaries regarding institutional roles and obligations are probably there for good reason. Many of our colleagues at the college engage in research, evaluation, and/or teaching that is highly satisfying to them and represents a vital contribution to the field of education. Indeed, one of our associates at the colleges raises serious and reasonable questions about the expectation that members of the education department must be continually involved with the schools to justify their role in the training of teachers. This individual sees the functions as quite distinct and concludes his obligations are in the area of scholarship, not the operation of the schools.

The position is a justifiable one and should be the source of neither quarrel nor comparison. For us, the distinction did not work. Both of us found it increasingly difficult to train teachers for an environment that was obviously undergoing major changes since we had last worked in it. Memory is selective, and we found there was a natural disposition to recall things that went well while screening out the many failures and the wear and tear that practicing teachers experience. Thus we concluded, quite independently, that our responsibilities would be better served by increased contact with the schools.

Having made such a decision, we were now obliged to work out the details of our relationship to the two institutions. Our role at the college was far easier to resolve. Here the culture provided a great deal of latitude for individuals to define the details of how they would go about performing their responsibilities. It is common practice to allow faculty to pursue specialized interests if they can provide support for replacements from outside sources. "Do your own thing" is a philosophy the colleges fully understand and for the most part support. Working out our role in the schools presented more formidable obstacles. The conventions were not at all clear and much of what we attempted had little precedent to guide it. One of the problems each of us faced in our efforts to collaborate with professional colleagues in the schools is that our knowledge of one another's work environments and demands is very uneven. We knew much more about the schools, having once served there, than many of our school counterparts knew about us. Some of our constant frustrations centered around persistent stereotypes of college staff, a lack of understanding about the needs (or self-interest) of the college, and the one-sided set of expectations about what we had to offer. Over the years, in a number of different projects, we consistently came up against the belief that the college had a huge pool of available resources that were just waiting to be conferred upon the schools. Even at the highest levels of leadership in the schools, we encountered the persistent assumption that there existed a large number of college staff and students whose time and energies could simply be shifted to the schools by virtue of our agreement that it was a good idea.

Not only was the existence of such resources an illusion, the belief that we would have had any control over them was an egregious overestimation of our power. It was difficult to convey that what we mainly had to offer was our desire to develop closer working relationships, and our willingness to use our influence to bring about this change. When such realistic assessments of our "power" were offered, they were usually attrib-uted to either undue modesty or limited interest in supporting a particular project. Most often, the schools expected us to *provide* resources rather than assuming that we would jointly accept responsibility for finding the support needed to *obtain* them. It was sometimes hard to convince some prospective collaborators that despite lighter teaching schedules, the col-lege staff was employed full-time and were simply not available to be assigned additional responsibilities in the schools. It was equally difficult to convince others that teacher trainees (e.g., observers, participants, student teachers, interns) were not readily available to work on such projects. These roles are not centrally assigned or controlled and most are involved in commitments that have lengthy histories and complex arrangements which are not subject to casual change. Diverting such "free" resources is not easy and is never accomplished swiftly. Convincing the schools that we needed to fund and/or create our own support for such supra-institutional efforts was often difficult. There remained an implicit belief that the college had resources to "contribute."

EMPLOYING ADDITIONAL HELP

A related problem was the issue of how such additional resources would be used. The schools are not always ready to make effective use of added personnel. Classroom teachers are also fully employed and do not always have the time, nor in some cases the inclination, to make the effort needed to skillfully integrate additional people into their activity. There is also the long tradition of teachers performing their function in complete isolation. Many have grown quite comfortable in that role and while administrators never seem to want to turn away "extra help," a number of teachers evidence no desire to have another adult in their classroom. Goodlad (1994) has noted the tendency and offered an explanation for it: "A consid-erable body of research leads not only to the conclusion that teachers work in considerable isolation, but also to the finding that many prefer to, and to the hypothesis that some choose teaching because it offers a degree of reclusiveness" (p. 99).

We share the sentiment about isolation but hold another view of its cause. It seems more likely that it grows out of teachers' recognition of their vulnerability to criticism. There is rarely a guarantee that what they do will be well received by either students or a classroom observer. A lesson that works successfully today can fail tomorrow or be received indifferently by another group in a later time period that same day. The knowledge of this can make teachers quite protective and cause them to avoid observers. Additionally, as we have noted throughout the book, most have been trained in a teaching culture that uses the Lone Ranger as a model, that is, teaching is something you do alone. That view is buttressed by the emphasis our culture places on individualism. Each person is encouraged to feel personally responsible for success or failure. As noted earlier, we have little experience of teaching as a corporate enterprise.

This emphasis on individual accountability is true of administrators as well and it is one of the main deterrents to alternative leadership models, such as school-based management. Because principals feel they personally will be held accountable for major problems in the school, many see the need to control rather than use such new approaches. They view them more as a danger than as an opportunity. Students from the college are seen as a much safer resource, and this serves to fuel the indiscriminate acceptance of such additional help even when its effective use is unlikely. What has been interesting to observe is the way that many of the same administrators who see parent help on a school-based management (SBM) team as threatening do not seem to understand or acknowledge that teachers have similar feelings about some of the help offered to them in the classroom. The unquestioning acceptance of whatever additional resources are available to "help" the instructional program can leave some teachers feeling victimized rather than enabled. We have seen schools that took in observers, participants, and student teachers all at once, in some vague belief that their presence could generally benefit the educational process. That may occur but it cannot be expected to happen automatically. The acceptance of such additional personnel by the leadership of the school should be accompanied by a plan which offers some reasonable assurance that they will be effectively used. Without a coherent design for how they will be integrated into the life of the school, their usefulness will remain more in the realm of appearance than reality.

Despite this, most school leadership remains fixated on getting more resources. Further, the implicit intent is usually to allow school staff to continue doing what they do, not to change it or experiment with different approaches. Seldom are additional resources employed to consider, let alone pursue alternative approaches. This results in using most additional resources to ease the burdens people are feeling, that is, to allow staff to continue doing the same things they have always done but to do them with greater ease. That is not always a worthy goal.

The colleges are as guilty as the schools in all this. They make placements with little thought or follow-up regarding their effectiveness for either the students or the school. The decisions are more often dictated by convenience rather than educational purpose. If greater cohesiveness is to be developed between school and college programs, more attention must be paid to the effective integration of resources sent from one institution to the other. A special effort will also have to be made to insure that the flow does not continue to be one way, as it traditionally has been. Personnel from the schools have a vital role to play in teacher training, but there is a need to create structures and opportunity for their effective use. For the most part, such structures do not currently exist and personnel from the schools have little or no involvement in college programs.

REDEFINING ROLES AND RESPONSIBILITIES

When roles have a lengthy history that have shaped and defined them, there is usually reasonable clarity about how they should be performed. Conversely, roles that are in the development process have fewer guidelines, and this ambiguity constitutes one of their greatest advantages, as well as their deepest drawback. The roles of the college faculty member in the collaborative process fit this definition of newness. It is not clearly defined, and hence it is rich in both opportunity and frustration.

An example of the opportunity end of the spectrum would be the experience of Dr. Fran Curcio, a mathematics educator from the college. She has made spectacular use of the site to enhance her own understanding of the schools, test the usefulness of new curriculum or materials, and refine certain approaches to teacher training. Moreover, she successfully translated this experience into research and writing activity that met the college's criteria for promotion.

On the other hand, Dr. Linda Catelli, a member of the Health and Physical Education faculty at Queens College, did an equally admirable job at the school—which has gone largely unrecognized. Her efforts represented what we felt was one of our greatest successes, and yet the college valued it little or not at all. For a period of 15 years she worked assiduously with the physical education faculty at the school to change what was essentially a recreational approach into a sound educational program. In the process, Dr. Catelli forged a small collaborative venture in which she and the school staff jointly trained new teachers on site. Further, she provided leadership in developing a well-designed curriculum that was responsive to the health, nutritional, physical, and recreational needs of the students. She reported her results at conferences and published accounts of her efforts in several journals. Yet it was nearly a decade before these efforts received even limited recognition at the college, though her teacher training program had wonderful implications for joining forces with the schools to improve the preparation and induction of novices to the profession. Almost the entire faculty at the college and most of the leadership of the school lack enthusiasm or understanding about what she has accomplished.

Part of the problem inherent in these contrasting pictures lies in the differential status accorded the two disciplines represented by the faculty members; however, this does not explain it all. There is a lack of interest in the change process itself, a limited recognition of the scarcity of successful models and the need to pay attention to efforts that work. Schools and colleges are frozen in the present. Little change occurs because both institutions are essentially organized to maintain continuity. As a result, there is little interest in and scant attention paid to what are considered experimental models, at least insofar as they imply change for the institution itself. The college absorbs such "change" by celebrating its receptivity to the unique efforts of individual staff members. This neatly avoids any consideration of their broader implications for reorganizing programs. The schools often view these efforts as a matter of personal style, an approach chosen by a select group of faculty members. Such small groups are accorded the same "freedom" an individual teacher would be given regarding instruction in their own classroom. In both instances, institutional change is contained and innovative efforts are reduced to a matter of personal choice, rather than an attempt to be responsive to the implicit demands of the institutional environment.

IMPROVING LEADERSHIP

In any effort similar to the one we have been involved in, leadership is the key. Yet in the conduct of such experimental endeavors, we have found that the requirements of the leadership role have been seriously underestimated. Too often those attempting change have put far too much confidence in the design or structure, that is, the mechanics of change. It is as if we were unconsciously repeating the error of making "teacher-proof" materials. There seems to be an implicit assumption that the plan and not the person is going to make the difference. In most cases, far more time and energy is spent on creating the design than is given to the choice of the leadership that will implement it. Such a mode of operation is tempting. Quality leadership is hard to find. Providing such leadership with the latitude needed to function effectively is even more difficult—it is far easier to create designs.

New York City, as with most large urban environments, has created a highly bureaucratized educational setting that places many limitations on the exercise of leadership. School principals are severely restricted in building a competent teaching staff since most teachers are centrally assigned to their school rather than chosen by them. Additionally, the sen-iority system built into the union contract means that younger staff mem-bers can be "bumped" by a senior teacher who is seeking a transfer. Nor does the principal have much choice about those who are assigned key responsibilities in the school. Most positions must be posted, and again seniority is a key factor. Nowhere is merit a major consideration. Though there are always informal means to flout some of these restrictions, their cumulative effect is to produce conformity and restrict the exercise of leadership. It is simply too wearing and time consuming to constantly wrestle with such an entrenched bureaucracy. Most change is thus con-fined to making rearrangements among a few variables that do not have severe restrictions imposed upon them. In essence, structural variables are rarely the focus of much attention, yet it is clear to most of us that they largely dictate the tenor and tone of the schools.

Education in our urban environments is likely to remain unrespon-sive to the needs of its diverse population of students until we find better ways of addressing this problem of providing leadership. School-based management has been put forward as one potential solution—that of broadening the leadership base by empowering parents and teachers. The approach holds some promise but it also has serious flaws. Accountability for decision-making continues to fall unevenly upon individuals in offi-cially sanctioned leadership roles. As one young principal told us, "The Board of Education is not going to fire the SBM committee when it believes a serious mistake has been made."

Conversely, the issue of empowering parents and teachers is never as simple as it appears. There is the issue of what is meant by empowerment; it should not be seen as simply a transfer of authority, nor should it result in an abdication of the principal's role. In urban schools that could serve to further undermine an already shaky leadership function. At its best, empowerment should mean a sharing of the ability to influence decision-making, but that must be accompanied by an attendant increase in re-sponsibility. When it is not, the system is in danger of separating risk from consequence. Such an occurrence would seem calculated to invite less reflection about choices, and empowerment, if it means anything, should mean a greater degree of thought about issues, an increased knowledge and understanding of the task at hand.

Very little attention has been paid to the need to make those involved in decision-making more knowledgeable. Most of the focus has been upon expanding the base of those who share power, the implicit assumption being that a broader base will lead to more equitable and responsive decisions. Yet anyone who has ever served on a committee knows that it is hardly a guarantor of an improved decision-making process. They have their advantages, but expediting decisions is not always one of them. A broader base of people involved in decisions can provide greater support, increased reflection, and a wider range of thinking about problems. However, this will not happen automatically, and for school-based management to succeed, more thought will have to be given to how responsibility as well as power can be shared. As a democratic nation, we rightly value the usefulness of locating decision-making close to those who will be affected by it; but as our historical experience with the Articles of Confederation has taught us, an excessive devotion to localizing power can also lead to paralysis and dysfunction. The schools still need leadership that is energetic, imaginative, and provides vision. Whatever structures we choose to employ should provide some reasonable assurance that they are likely to promote progress and not simply checks on the exercise of power. The latter is a necessary — but not sufficient — condition for promoting the welfare of the institution.

None of this is meant to imply that leadership — as it is currently exercised in the schools — is not in need of serious scrutiny. Indeed, the main argument put forward in this chapter is the need to attract, train, and support an improved quality of leadership. We simply note the dangers inherent in some of the proposed solutions and suggest the need to test approaches for the specific improvements they are purported to offer.

MAKING CHANGE

The way that any institution is punished for mistakes has vast implications for the amount of risk-taking that will be attempted. It has been our experience that the college has a wider latitude for mistakes than the schools. That is probably because the consequences are neither as dire nor as immediate as they are in the schools. Parents respond with alacrity and anger to circumstances they perceive as damaging to children who have not reached maturity and are not fully able to defend themselves. Thus, the margin for error is probably more narrow in the schools and results in less experimentation or change than is warranted.

There are other circumstances that have produced a lack of receptivity for change in the schools. Educational innovation is a seriously flawed process in this nation. Since the 1960s the general approach has been to promote the new by denigrating the old. That has led to vastly exaggerated claims for what some of these untested new techniques or materials could actually produce. One unintended consequence of this approach has been its propensity for organizing active opposition to the change. Another has been the tendency to measure success against these bloated claims, frequently leading to the abandonment of useful approaches whose main fault was their proponents had overpromised what they could deliver. The process bears interesting similarities to our political campaigns and subsequent efforts at governance. Here too our leaders overpromise and frequently end up scorned for their inability to live up to the false expectations they have created.

Another problem is that there can be a good deal of educational chicanery in the promotion of products or materials presumably created to support new approaches. There are vast commercial considerations that attach themselves to issues in literature (whole language), mathematics (manipulative materials), or science (hands-on curricula). There is also the opportunity for career enhancement that comes from being a major or early proponent of a new approach. And there is the constant danger of innovative elitism, a kind of avant-garde posturing conducted more for the attention it attracts than for any reasonable prospect of improving student learning.

Too often, educational innovation has been the victim of commercialism, career-enhancing tactics, or the creation of excessive expectations. It has also suffered from the myth that ideas or practices which proved productive elsewhere are easily transferable to different sites. However, research has demonstrated that they are not, that it is people who make the difference. Again, this myth is probably rooted in the excessive confidence that has been placed in the design, technique, or materials rather than the personnel who employ them. Our consistent experience has been that effective change requires vision, capable leadership, and the strong support of the staff who will implement the ideas. Often insufficient consideration is given to these important factors.

Promoting intelligent innovative efforts remains the key to improving the way our educational institutions functions. Good organizations should seek ways to make change before they become dysfunctional. Unfortunately, in education there are not always clear incentives for doing so — traditional practice often remains both isolated and insulated enough to continue on its normal course. Because most research *about* the schools is not conducted by personnel *from* the schools, education has a poor record of applying what has been learned. One of the legacies of this impoverished connection between application and research is that we frequently repeat errors and just as frequently ignore successful efforts that might have broader implications.

DEALING WITH DIFFICULTIES

Conducting a collaboration can be demanding. Such efforts can tolerate mistakes but not failure, and major mishaps represent a serious threat to their continuation. This is especially true at the beginning, when the project is most vulnerable, but it remains a threat throughout. Those of us involved in the LAMS collaboration often heard of an earlier effort by Queens College to collaborate closely with an elementary school in one of the districts in the borough. The effort had concluded some 18 years ago, and yet on three separate occasions within the past 5 years, questions about the college's contribution to the school were raised by personnel from that district during large group meetings.

At the time, the School of Education at Queens College had a faculty that numbered more than 150 full-time staff and some 50 adjuncts. There were never more than five faculty members assigned to this project, yet concerns about the quality or their commitment were expressed as if they were typical of an entire faculty. Beyond that, the details of the actual contribution of the college staff were a matter of some dispute and varied with the individuals who were questioned. Nonetheless, almost 20 years later, those of us who had embarked on a similar effort found ourselves the object of negative stereotypes engendered by a single, small prior effort where we had had no involvement. The circumstances are reported to make the point that taking risks can have harmful consequences, merited or unmerited, even years later. These are not cost-free exercises and no one is protected against making mistakes, small or large. Indeed, the only assurance is that some mistakes will be made.

An example of how such mistakes can occur was an experience we had in helping reorganize they school into houses and interdisciplinary teams. The assignment of faculty to houses and the formation of the teams were very skillfully conducted. There was a great deal of faculty involvement and a maximum degree of choice was provided. Teams were formed by combining formal and informal means to assure that they consisted of people who truly wanted to work together. Once formed, the teams were offered wide latitude regarding the extent and type of "teaming" that took place. The division of the school into houses was handled with similar skill and equally positive results.

The planning and organization involved to accomplish this took the better part of a year and was conducted with great care. The last item to be addressed was the assignment of three assistant principals, one to each of the houses that had been formed. We gave little thought to this and made no special plan for working out such assignments. There were three assistant principals and three houses. It seemed like a simple accommodation and we accepted the suggestion by the three assistant principals that they would meet, work out the assignments, and report back to us.

The result was not as smooth as one would have hoped. In retrospect, we probably should have anticipated the kind of disagreements that arose.

We did not take into account the fact that there was a history here. There always is. Some of the assistant principals felt they related better to certain teachers and that it should have been evident to their colleagues that they were the logical choice to supervise them. There had also been trade-offs in the past — responsibilities assumed or avoided by one or the other that were factored into their thinking about who should step aside and allow the other their preference, because it was owed. Once disagreements surfaced, it was harder to get the agreements we needed. Though these were eventually worked out in a reasonably satisfactory way, it was clear that by ignoring this "minor" decision we had courted real danger. In effect, the structure of the houses and teams was so appealing to the vast majority of staff that it allowed us to overcome what might have become a serious obstacle to effective implementation. In subsequent endeavors, we learned to make fewer assumptions about what would require intensive planning and what would flow more smoothly.

We faced similar problems in an effort to implement a student advisory program for the school. Again, the planning and preparation prior to implementation was carefully done. The rationale for student advisories was carefully put forward and training was provided for the full staff. Key staff members were enabled to visit sites where effective advisory programs were being conducted. Much that would help get the program off to a successful start had been done.

What our experience did not prepare us for was the fact that because the nature of the activity was new, many veteran teachers would find themselves reduced to the role of novices. The advisory thrust teachers into a small group structure (10 students) whose main purpose was to afford students the opportunity to explore concerns and examine needs. Some found that when content was removed, they no longer had a role they could understand or feel comfortable in. Despite the preparation for the open-ended nature of the advisory, a small number of teachers found that the absence of subject matter robbed their role of its traditional meaning. That can be a problem for advisory programs — it was for ours.

Some of this could be attributed to the complications that arise when experienced teachers find themselves in circumstances that make them feel like beginners. Only time and experience will provide the skill and confidence needed, but this requires individuals to remain committed to the effort through that period. Some would not, and a reluctant mentor is a contradiction in terms. As a result, the advisory become voluntary and a number of staff dropped out.

The misfortune for students was compounded by the fact that the majority of those who felt uncomfortable in the role were seventh- and eighth-grade teachers. The adolescents in these grades perhaps had the greatest need for an adult mentor. Conversely, the teachers at these grade levels had the greatest difficulty in adjusting to a role where the traditional curriculum content was not the sole issue. As had been carefully explained, the necessary role was not one of a therapist but that of a "good parent" who helped provide support during a challenging period in a young person's life. We remain convinced that advisories are highly beneficial to students and represent one of the best ways for teachers to develop keen insight into the actual needs of the adolescents that they are presumably educating. Such insight would inform both the curriculum and instructional practice and could represent one of the better staff development exercises in which teachers could engage. Unfortunately for our project, the experience has been a very uneven one, with the students and teachers who would stand to benefit most deprived of a useful opportunity.

WHAT MAKES GOOD SCHOOLS: SOME VITAL PRINCIPLES

It would be an interesting exercise to try and determine what people feel constitutes a good school. Our experience has been that "good" is measured on a comparative scale. A school is good if students are performing better than most of their peers. Urban school systems suffer a great deal from such comparisons — and unfairly so, in our judgment. One should measure a good school or school system not simply by what it does but by what it can be. Given the resources, support, and levels of student ability, how could the staff have used them to accomplish better things? You measure achievement not simply by comparison to others but against a good objective analysis of what is the best you can be when provided with superior financial resources that result in better staffing or lower pupil/ teacher ratios.

Too often we end up measuring educational progress against the mundane and unimaginative. We have visited — and have encouraged teachers to visit — a number of suburban school districts that are doing interesting things. We have found some to be far less impressive than their circumstances might allow. Staff rightfully boast of student achievement but do not always consider what they might be able to accomplish. Too often such high achievement districts are looked to as the standard when they are simply the beneficiaries of better motivated students, superior resources, and more active community support.

Student growth and performance is a key issue. That should cause us to examine those things that contribute to the kind of school climate which encourages such growth and enables students to make the best use of the abilities they have been given. There are, it seems to us, some key ideas that recommend themselves for consideration. One is developing a climate of thought in the school. That climate must extend to both students and staff. Students should be encouraged to participate actively in their own education. To do this will require changes in the structure of our schools. The professional staff must be provided with time to think and reflect about how this should be done. In most situations the school day begins when students arrive and ends when they leave. The structure provides time to teach but no time for staff to meet, discuss, reflect, and plan with regularity. We will not break out of what many feel is a sterile educational mold until time is provided for such planning and reflection. A staff that is not engaged in continuous reflection and analysis is far less likely to develop such traits in their students.

Another important issue is developing an ethos of caring in the schools. Following World War II and the trend toward economies of scale, our educational institutions became too large and too impersonal. There is a need to humanize these environments so that student and staff do not feel lost. We attempted to do this by creating houses, teaching teams, and advisories. The effort was to create units small enough to relate to one another even within the larger environment. The houses broke down a school of 1350 students into units of 450. The teams provided a cluster of teachers who worked with the same 125 students. The advisories matched one adult with ten young people. The intent was to establish feelings of community, a sense of connectedness and belonging that would translate into a climate of concern for one another. Such arrangements have important consequences for both personal and academic growth. Our experience with social units as disparate as families or gangs should long ago have taught us the enormous need our young people have to feel cared for, to believe that they belong. Schools ignore such data and its implications for organizational structure at their own peril.

A third issue is that of empowering students. Critics have long complained of the essentially passive nature of the role assigned to the learner in our schools. We need to tap the power to contribute that students have demonstrated in programs of peer mediation, community service, and peer tutoring. Many are not only ready and able, but they need to contribute if they are to grow. We have found that for some students, only greater freedom and deeper involvement in their own education will enable them to learn. For these the choice is empowerment or intellectual stagnation. The better schools are not afraid to empower their students.

Finally, we believe good schools are those whose program is informed by a vital educational vision. That vision should be comprehensive enough to inspire great effort to attain its goals and specific enough to guide those who are pursuing them. Far too many of our schools have no special sense of purpose. Education can have a sense of adventure for both students and teachers when a clear and exciting vision of what can be accomplished is provided.

The issues noted above are of paramount importance. Schools that attend to them are better places for students to be. This goes beyond the middle school philosophy we have been emphasizing. These issues lie at the heart of what a good school should be. One of the things that has long concerned us is that the schools for the most privileged children in our nation have long provided such benefits. The benefits of small group settings, individualized instruction, houses, and personal access to the adults who do the teaching have long been recognized. Their value has not been lost on the prestigious private schools and colleges that educate the elite of our society. Most of these schools have chosen to remain small and place a heavy emphasis upon the quality of the interaction among students and between students and teachers. Thus it is common for such private schools or even for elite universities like Harvard or Yale to organize their students into smaller units ("houses" or "colleges"). That most of our large public junior and senior high schools do not do so is surely not because these younger students are any less in need of intimacy, security, and greater access to the adults who model learning for them.

Deborah Meier, principal of an alternative, innovative secondary school in East Harlem, has framed the problem well:

> A few years back I gave a speech to our students about how special we all were — our school, our staff, and, of course, our students.
>
> Afterwards, a youngster came up to me to ask, quietly, "How come if this school is so special, you accepted me?"
>
> That question has haunted me . . . The trouble has been that the characteristics of good schools have only been present in the schools for society's "special kids" — the most affluent or the intellectually gifted. . . . But the characteristics of the best schools — their pride in their youngsters (high expectation), the vigorous and challenging quality of their curriculum (high content), and the myriad ways in which they nurture and care (high support) are precisely those that have been stripped away from the schools our most disadvantaged youngsters attend. It's as though we dared them to succeed in an environment most unlikely to support their personal and intellectual growth. (quoted in Lewis, 1990, p. 5)

Meier goes on to ask, "Why couldn't the schools for all our young people be special?" (p. 5). It is a good question. Some of the points addressed in this chapter represent part of the answer. We know some of the things we have to do. What we need to develop is the type of consensus among those concerned that will allow us to mount the sustained effort needed to implement them.

CHAPTER 10

Our Policy Recommendations and Our Ongoing Questions About Collaboration

The major premise underlying the Queen College–Louis Armstrong Middle School collaboration is the idea that no one institution alone can succeed in effecting fundamental educational change. Responsibility for school reform should not be shared in a linear fashion with schools of education assuming responsibility for the preparation of staff and then turning over the task of teacher induction to the public school. The job of school development belongs to both college and public school personnel, beginning with professional preparation courses and continuing in the schools with inservice programs.

The policy recommendations we make come from our experience with collaboration. Some refer directly to ways in which institutions can best work with each other while others relate to the role of collaboration in educational change.

POLICY RECOMMENDATIONS

Recommendation 1: Make Provision for Teaching the Skills of Collaboration.

Collaboration involves skills that can be learned. In this era of greater collaboration (school–college collaboration, school-based management, team teaching, and collaborative instruction for inclusion) it becomes imperative that preservice and inservice programs give attention to developing the skills of working together.

The task of collaboration is no simple matter. It calls for an ability to be open to ideas that may run counter to one's philosophy. It asks that participants understand that there is a gap between idea generation and idea implementation. For someone to state a point of view and to expect that it will be readily translated into practice is to be naive about how change occurs. As true teaching is not simply spouting information, change is not brought about by telling the other party what they need to know. It doesn't work that way. Verbalizing is not necessarily connecting, and it is connectedness we need if a joint effort is to have any success. Collaboration often falters when a participant presents a sound proposal only to see it shot down because there has been a failure to understand that simply presenting an approach will not work unless people have had a chance to think through and accept the significance of the new idea.

The practice of collaboration has not been part of either the public school or college ethos. Teachers and professors are unaccustomed to working with others and — as we have noted elsewhere — time has rarely been made available for people to share their thinking. The way public schools and colleges are organized keeps professionals apart rather than encouraging joint efforts. In most schools teachers are isolated in their classrooms, while at the university professors deal almost exclusively on an individual basis in their particular area of expertise.

Steps should be taken to find ways to support the process of collaboration. Students, professors, teachers, and administrators all need to become familiar with the group process, to develop an understanding of how role shapes behavior, to recognize the importance of listening to the other person's point of view, to be given experiences in working with those who have another perspective, and to be provided opportunities to collaborate with others on projects. In addition, time for dialogue needs to be provided and structures established which facilitate professional interaction.

What is the expected outcome of such efforts at collaboration? We believe that learning is as much a communal enterprise as it is an individual one, and that more will be gained from using both modes. It is true that the individual receives and processes data in ways that are tied to personal gifts and his or her unique set of interests. However, we are also social animals. Much of what we learn takes place in a communal environment and is responsive to that kind of setting. Schools take too little formal notice of the importance of the peer groups in much of the learning that takes place. The phenomenon is little studied, and rarely are efforts made to take advantage of its positive potential. Collaboration is an issue for learners at all age levels. It is a tool that can be employed interorganizationally as well as interpersonally.

Recommendation 2: Build Strong Linkages Between Colleges and Public Schools.

Collaboration between college and public school should not be viewed as a one-way street with university personnel coming to the schools to provide the panacea for the school's ills. Rather, bridges between the two institutions need to be erected, with the faculties of both institutions teaching at the other's site and with students from both school and college finding opportunities to meet on campus and at the school building. Boundaries between institutions, as with countries, are where differences and conflict start; bridges, on the other hand, increase the likelihood of mutual understanding. Barriers are breached when public school faculty join with professors to teach college courses, when professors and public school faculty together write articles for publication and present findings at professional conferences. The continual aim is to blur roles, with professors taking on the tasks of public school teachers and teachers experiencing what it is to be a professor.

A large move toward bridge-building occurs when schools of education in cooperation with boards of education develop professional development schools. Just as there are teaching hospitals to help prepare doctors and to give practicing physicians ongoing contact with current findings in medicine, so should there be professional development schools to prepare teachers and to allow ongoing contact with public schools. These professional development schools can also serve as research and development centers comparable to those which exist in industry. These centers could provide time for reflection, encourage accurate problem identification, and facilitate the gathering of data. Such centers need to be continually operating, since schools are institutions in constant flux. Their function must be multi-dimensional in nature, and their task is to be responsive to the changing set of difficulties facing our schools.

It should be noted that if model programs are to be implemented in the professional development center, then staff needs to be carefully chosen. If the professional development school is to be viewed as a training ground for new teachers, then inservice personnel with whom they work should represent high-quality teaching. Transfer rights and seniority should give way to superior qualification as the criterion for staff selection. None of this is meant to imply that prospective teachers will be kept away from problems that may exist in difficult schools. It is to state that the foundation of teacher strength, as with a child growing up, comes from early positive experience.

Recommendation 3: Modify the College Reward System to Give Greater Recognition to Service in Schools, and Recruit Faculty Who Show Promise of Having Special Ability to Work in the Field.

The college's reward system needs to expand to give recognition to those professors who evince particular skills in working with schools. Encouragement and guidance should be given to faculty on how to utilize the school as a laboratory to increase knowledge. As part of the college's recruitment and hiring process, attention should be given to those who give indication of an ability to combine work in the field with a capacity to do research.

As it presently exists, the college reward system encourages abstract experimentation. Exploration that culminates in quantitative data is what carries weight in the minds of those who distribute rewards. What pleases college authorities most is precisely what public school people see as useless. The perennial comment of teachers is that college professors are too theoretical and what they produce is of little value to the classroom instructor. Educators with skills in shaping schools and with interest in doing so also suffer from the low status accorded schools of education, because the latter have not seen fit to produce research along the lines valued by college administration. This view of what constitutes appropriate professorial activity causes enormous difficulty in recruiting college faculty to work in schools. If promotion and tenure decisions are to be made on the basis of a narrow definition of knowledge production, then professors will likely direct their energies elsewhere than at the schools.

The values of pure research are large. But the contributions of those who perform the creative act of influencing school environments should also be recognized. The publish or perish syndrome that now dominates the college campus is a surprisingly narrow vision of how professorial staff can contribute to the broader community. It limits other efforts and punishes divergent interests, which can range from teaching to community organization and to working in the schools. Considering that the latter is such a vital contributor to the life of the university itself—let alone the larger society—it is difficult to understand the lack of support offered to qualitative efforts in this arena.

Recommendation 4: Provide Recognition for Public School Personnel Who Make Special Contributions to Teacher Preparation and Teacher Induction.

Recognition is in short supply in public schools. Most teachers perform in isolation, and the only occasion for any kind of spotlight is the commission of error. Increased opportunity must be found for teachers to share their experience and expertise. Their use as resources in college classes, in other schools, and in their own school—and the acknowledgment of teacher ideas and achievement—should become regular practice.

Recognition should also be accorded public school personnel who make direct contributions to teacher preparation and teacher induction by

serving as cooperating teachers, mentors, or supervisors of student teachers. This recognition could include selection as clinical professors and
identification as such in college catalogs, tuition waivers, compensation
for extra time, inclusion in conference presentations, co-writing articles
with professors, invitations to participate in research projects, and support
to attend professional conferences. These ways represent some possibilities
of acknowledging the value of the public school staff's role. Recognition of
this contribution reinforces the idea that teacher development is ongoing
and involves the efforts of people from both institutions. Moreover, such
recognition could take the form of providing release time for those with
special talent to contribute to other endeavors related to the task of educating our young people. There is always the danger that such "recognition"
will end up tempting those rewarded to seek more prestigious or better
paying assignments. That has happened, and will continue to do so. A
better way to address the dilemma is to provide those who are able and
interested with the opportunity to do both, to perform differentiated tasks
that satisfy both their desire to teach young children and communicate to
other adults some of the things they have learned about the process.

Recommendation 5: Give Priority to and Broaden the Scope of Staff Development Programs.

The importance of a comprehensive, thoughtful, and ongoing staff development program cannot be overstated. Teachers begin their professional
lives as incomplete products. Four or even five years of preparation do not
give teachers the many skills and insights needed. In addition, teaching,
like medicine, is a profession that calls for its members to be refreshed and
updated as new ideas and materials come to the fore. School staffs are also
faced with the necessity of adapting to changing societal circumstances.
The dysfunctional family, the AIDS epidemic, and the increasing segregation of schools give schools and teachers problems to deal with that did not
exist 20 years ago.

    In the absence of a meaningful, stimulating staff development pro-
gram, school goals most often focus on institutional survival rather than
on institutional growth. An essential ingredient for effective staff development is time for professionals to reflect on their experiences. Inservice
learning restricted to monthly afterschool conferences does little to enhance teacher growth. The services of a knowledgeable outside observer
can help overcome the limitations of experience that offer only a narrow
range of the possibilities available to professionals.

    Preservice and inservice education limited to teaching methodology
and to classroom management gives an incomplete picture of the scope of

responsibility faced by teachers. Teacher development needs to take into account the totality of the school and to deal with such questions as the following: What are the best ways to work with paraprofessional and nonprofessional personnel? How can parent and community involvement be obtained? What support services are available to the teacher? What is the teacher's role with regard to unions and professional associations? How can we work more cooperatively together?

Teacher growth cannot be left to chance. If teachers are not to fall prey to stagnation, time and resources need to be available to provide the means and encouragement for continued learning. Collaborative endeavors can play a large role in promoting teacher development.

Recommendation 6: Plan Comprehensively for Educational Change, Taking Into Account the Culture, Climate, Personnel, and Working Arrangements in the School.

Proposals that focus only on a single aspect of education will fall short of the desired effect. For example, raising standards (a favorite remedy) in particular subject matter areas will not be really productive unless teacher skills in these areas are also upgraded. Similarly, any attempt to imprint a middle school philosophy onto an existing school structure — without giving consideration to the particular characteristics of the institution — will lead to frustration. No matter how sound the proposed approach, it is essential that such factors as teacher strengths and weaknesses, organizational structures (formal and informal), attitudes of parents and the community, and school climate be taken into account.

There is also a need for recognition that school reform efforts will prove insufficient unless they are accompanied by concurrent restructuring of teacher education programs to insure an ongoing supply of well-prepared teachers. Undergraduate teacher education programs are inadequate for giving prospective teachers thorough preparation. A graduate internship can provide experience that extends beyond the single classroom. By extending the boundaries of the intern's experience, the teacher-to-be gains familiarity with a number of teaching styles, has opportunity to learn about the community and parent body, and finds out about the roles of counselors, social workers, custodial staff, and paraprofessionals. An internship gives newcomers to the profession a chance to broaden and deepen knowledge, to identify a teaching style with which they feel most comfortable, and to gain confidence.

Teacher preparation courses should no longer be confined to a campus. From the beginning these classes need to provide experiences in the field. The rigid boundaries separating public school and college do not allow prospective teachers to gain as full a picture as possible of their future roles. The focus on field experience will have the benefit of keeping professors apprised of developments in the schools and will provide for early involvement of practitioners in the process of preparing teachers. When we speak of such field-based assignments, we do not mean the traditional practice of simply placing trainees in the schools. We are speaking of comprehensive, interinstitutional arrangements that give these assignments meaning and purpose. Trainees require supervision and guidance that will help them profit from the experience. Simple placement does not translate into growth.

It is predictable that the attempt to achieve school change will fail unless there is recognition that solutions will not be immediate, that the task is complex, and that modification of teacher preparation programs also be part of the reform effort. The last goal will not be easy. The self-perception of the college staff is that they are not only open to change, but are indeed change agents. Such assumptions cause one to consistently look outward rather than inward when the issue of change becomes a serious topic of conversation. Altering this traditional view of where change needs to take place represents a formidable challenge.

In considering what needs to be done, there is the temptation to put wishes forward as policy recommendations. Public school–college collaborations would profit greatly if administrative leadership could be stabilized and interest in the project from top officials could be maintained. But wishes for stability will not stop people from seeking advancement, nor will it provide funds that have been limited by shrinking budgets. Thus, we have tried to confine ourselves to recommendations that we feel would serve collaboratives well. We have also tried to restrict what we are suggesting to elements over which those engaged in a collaborative arrangement have some control.

QUESTIONS WE ASK OURSELVES AND OUR RESPONSES

During the course of the collaboration, questions arose that nag us until this day. Periodically we return to these questions, seeking more complete responses. They include the following.

Question 1: Why Has the Collaboration Been Less Effective Than We Would Have Liked in Impacting the College's Teacher Education Program?

What happened is that the teacher education program at the college has remained substantially the same. To be sure, a handful of professors have succeeded in finding a laboratory for exploration at LAMS. There are those who teach courses on site, frame research that focuses on life in schools, interact with school staff on a regular basis, and have found much material to bring back to their campus classes.

But most professors continue to teach their individual courses utilizing textbooks as the primary source, doing research distant from schools, and having little contact with the day-to-day life of teachers. From our vantage point, this kind of teacher education can be compared to preparing medical students without encouraging them to have contact with patients or hospitals. Some of the courses can — and perhaps even should — be conducted in such isolation. That the vast majority of professors should choose to remain in such isolation, however, raises serious questions in our mind.

Public schools have long been criticized for imperviousness to change as evidenced, for example, by the fact that the junior high schools of today are very much like the same institutions of the 1920s. Teacher education has been no less resistant to change, with current preparation programs little different from what existed decades ago. Comfort and fear have been among the major deterrents to change in teacher education. There is little motivation to modify preparation programs when professors are assured of a steady flow of students seeking to become teachers, when the first goal of professional activity continues to be publication and a two- or three-day teaching schedule that gives the time to write, and when teaching exclusively at the college relieves instructors of the stresses and strains of school life. In maintaining a traditional approach to teacher preparation, professors are able to make pronouncements freely about education uncontaminated by the complexities and uncertainties of actual schools. Some professors find satisfaction and comfort in playing the role of sage.

Fear too supports maintaining the status quo. For professors to move beyond teaching courses on campus means putting their philosophies and abilities on the line, a situation that might well cause anxiety. It is far less threatening to deliver views from the safety of the college classroom. Since a considerable number of faculty have had little experience in working with public schools, or, in other cases, have not been in the field for many years, it is little wonder that there is reluctance to break away from the campus-based class as the core of teacher preparation.

The workings of the college reward system have also served to inhibit change in teacher education. Since writing for publication continues as the major — if not the only — criteria for promotion and tenure, a teaching schedule of 9 hours a week is conducive to personal research. Commitment to the field calls for a much larger expenditure of time, reducing the hours available for writing. So long as publication remains the college's priority, little incentive exists to modify preparation programs to integrate field experiences with courses on campus. Teacher-education program inertia is reinforced by recruitment and hiring policies that seek out people with publication records rather than those with experience in working in the field.

We have come to realize that teacher education programs will continue as they have for the most part, unless college leadership gives concrete evidence that they support the integration of the campus classroom with the world of schools. In the meantime, we have gained some solace and gratification from the fact that the collaboration has provided a laboratory for some professors, that some college classes are taught at the school site, and that there are other faculty who search out opportunity to give their undergraduates direct experience in schools.

Question 2: How Can We Measure the Worth of the School-College Collaboration?

Periodically, we pause to ask ourselves what has been the value of the collaboration. In our self-examination we seek not to ignore the formal evaluations of the collaboration which have been conducted, but to reach further to explore areas that are less subject to quantitative assessment. We are comforted by the positive recognition the collaboration has received in such books as Gene Maeroff's *School and College: Partnerships in Education* (1983) and Ernest Boyer's *High School* (1983) and from the U.S. Department of Education's designation of the school as exemplary. It is also reassuring to note the Board of Education's Office of Educational Evaluation report, which indicated the school's above average performance in academic areas, its excellent attendance, and its ability to attract increasing numbers of applicants for a limited number of openings (in the 1993–94 school year 3000 applicants for some 350 places). Still, the recognition that has been gained is neither the real measure nor the only purpose of the collaboration. For example, we see useful, innovative programs like Camp Armstrong, Early Bird, and the School and Community Museum, activities that have been institutionalized and are now part of the school operation, and feel they have potential in other settings. We would like to see them gain even more widespread use than they have. Similarly, considerable effort has gone into developing an ethos of openness and cooperation at the school, which may escape an evaluator's attention, but it has added immeasurably to the success the school has experienced. Teachers at LAMS have opened their classroom to a steady flow of visitors. They expect student teachers, graduate interns, professors, and others to come to their classes to observe and to discuss what they have seen. Ongoing contact between the public school and the college has become institutionalized and college staff are viewed as an integral part of the school environment. It is the willingness of staff to take the risk of exposing themselves to other people and ideas that has allowed many successful ideas to be implemented.

Another area of importance that is hard to measure is the creation of a school climate that has encouraged staff to go beyond action to thinking about what is being attempted. To an increasing extent, teachers give time to reflection about ideas that are put forward before any efforts at implementation are made.

Key efforts have centered around the implementation of middle school concepts. From a school that started as a typical junior high school complete with 42-minute periods taught by specialists, we have moved to an institution characterized by advisory programs, interdisciplinary instruction, cooperative learning, house plans, and team organization. Perhaps most important is the widespread acceptance that LAMS is a school in process, rather than a finished product. Such a perspective translates into less acceptance of the status quo and a greater tendency to look for ways to improve. We are wary of making definitive statements about positive school change, knowing how ephemeral such progress can be. However, we can say with confidence that as a result of the collaboration, LAMS is a different (and, we hope, better) school than it would have been without the involvement of the college.

Question 3: How Do We Go About Creating a School Environment in Which Staff Engage in Planning and Reflection About What They Are Doing?

When either of the authors has returned from a visit to a school in which progress is being made, invariably one of our comments has been, "One good thing about the school is that people get together to think." Most commonly, schools operate as "doing" places rather than as organizations where staff ponder ideas and give thought to the ramifications and consequences of proposed actions. A major obstacle in the path of reflection is the pressure for immediate solutions. A rash of student fights, chronic failure to do homework, or poor scores on tests and the result is the same — a marshaling of forces to produce a quick response. Rarely does faculty pause to consider possible reasons for problems, to gather data, or to pose alternative solutions. Almost never is there any recognition of the fact that problems may have multiple causes, resulting from many influences and emanating from dozens of possible sources, and that school or staff action needs to be preceded by thinking.

Another factor inhibiting thinking is the lack of time for staff to meet.

At the outset we recognized the need for organizing the school to give staff increased opportunity to exchange views. We obtained permission in the original school design for children to be dismissed early one afternoon a month to allow faculty to get together. Although of some help, this meager allotment of additional time has hardly proved sufficient for providing the hours needed for in-depth exploration of school matters. The way schools almost everywhere are organized demonstrates that little importance is placed on teacher planning, review, and evaluation of their efforts. Unlike industry, where companies, as a matter of course, include retreats, planning sessions, and think tanks, schools plod along, always working to master the present and giving little attention to the future. It would not be totally invalid to assess a school's effectiveness in terms of the time available for communication and thinking among staff.

One of our goals as directors of the collaboration has been to expand opportunities for staff reflection. We've initiated a series of brown-bag lunches, where invited teachers share views on such subjects as dealing with heterogeneous groups, developing alternative approaches to student assessment, and implementing cooperative learning. These gatherings are held on site in a Queens College meeting room, which has become a place for relaxed talk and idea exchange.

Each day — as part of the daily routine of the college director — a walk around the building is conducted to provide support for interns and student teachers and to answer questions. These trips around the school are not primarily for the purpose of looking for problems or even for finding effective instructional practices. These wanderings give staff occasion to raise concerns and share ideas or questions they may have. We have found that teachers are eager to talk to someone who shows interest and is in a nonevaluative role. A casual inquiry can lead to exploration that goes beyond immediate solutions and to in-depth consideration of problems. A simple "How's the class doing?" can be the launching pad to share concern about a vexing situation. On a recent occasion one teacher replied, "I'd like to change my approach this year. I feel I've been too controlling. I'd like to put more responsibility in the hands of students. But I'm not sure of how to go about it. I worry about things going wrong. I want to make sure the curriculum gets covered." This brief interchange resulted in meetings over lunch, initial plans to establish small groups in the class, and periodic sessions to assess progress. It needs to be noted that interactions of this sort can occur only if mutual trust has been established.

Habits form as a result of repeated practice. The habit of thinking is no different. If reflection is to become a regular part of the approach of school staff to teaching, they need frequent opportunity to explore their responses to classroom situations. We have found that asking interns to maintain daily journals about their school experience has been of enormous value in ingraining the habit of reflection. By writing about what occurs they see things more clearly than if thoughts were allowed to remain vague and unspecified. Writing strengthens the thinking response to situations. This practice of keeping journals has been carried over by former interns who have become regularly assigned classroom teachers. The journal, as one teacher put it, "is like having someone else to talk to about what's happening in class."

Opportunity for thoughtful exchanges increases if space is made available for people to meet. The fact that the Queens College collaboration has a classroom size office encourages people to come together to share ideas. We have since made the availability of such space a condition for establishing a collaboration at a school site. Our experience has indicated that such working space is needed for the many informal and formal meetings that sustain the larger endeavor.

Actions propelled by limited prior planning require little expenditure of energy. Thinking is hard and takes effort. It seems a paradox that curriculum discussions often focus on the need to develop critical thinking skills in students and yet little opportunity has been provided for school staffs to practice and implement their own powers of critical thinking. If a school is to maintain forward momentum, then reflection needs to be encouraged. College faculty can facilitate the reflection effort by asking questions, by active listening, and by suggesting books and articles that prod staff to examine teaching practices.

Question 4: What Are the Factors That Have Allowed the Collaboration to Continue For So Long a Period of Time?

Past experience tells us that collaborations between universities and public schools are short-lived. The Queens College–Louis Armstrong Middle School project, contrary to what might be expected, has prevailed for almost 20 years with little indication that its demise is in the immediate offing. A number of factors have contributed to the collaboration's longevity, none more important than the fact that the authors have been active participants from the moment the project was conceived to the present. We know that circumstances that compel people to leave cannot be controlled. It remains a fact, however, that longevity helps, and rapid turnover hurts efforts such as these.

From the start we have operated as advisors, facilitators, implementers, resource locators, staff recruiters, and as partners in policy formulation and decision-making. Although the quality of our involvement has varied over the years depending on the attitude of the particular school principal, the development of the school has always included college personnel as key players. We have been established as part and parcel of the school's operation. The idea of the college as a fixture at Louis Armstrong has been further strengthened by the presence of a number of faculty who have been working in the school for periods ranging from 10 to 15 years. With the passage of time (particularly in the early years, when public school personnel were assessing the college faculty in terms of their authenticity, their sincerity, and the value that would or would not result from the collaboration), university personnel have come to be viewed as sources of ideas, materials, and support. The professional lives of teachers and professors have become intertwined as they have co-written articles, co-presented at conferences, and co-taught courses. The ongoing presence of the project leaders, the sustained involvement of a cadre of professors, and the positive response of faculty to college participation from both those who began with the school and those who joined the staff (having been interns or student teachers) have brought project stability and an attitude that says, "The college is supposed to be here. It's part of the school."

The stability represented by the continued involvement of familiar professorial faces would not have been possible had it not been accompanied by the development of trust that allowed the different personal and professional worlds to overlap. But beyond trust there needed to be the feeling that the collaboration has proved helpful. Even more than the creation of a wholesome professional atmosphere, what has contributed most to the continuance of the collaboration has been the school's success, the perception that it represents a center of educational excellence to which the college has been a major and essential contributor.

Another element nurturing the collaboration has been the backing of parents, politicians, and community groups. We recognized from the start, both for reasons emanating from principle and from a desire to be effective, that there was a need to gain the involvement and support of other groups. In the beginning we worked with union representatives in the staffing of the school; we welcomed and encouraged the participation of parents; we joined with local groups and politicians to develop a school design that would serve the needs of the community. The effort to maintain the support of the various constituencies continues to this day. Proof of our effectiveness in this regard is evidenced by the fact that whenever there is even a whisper that the collaboration might be ended, parents, politicians, and community representatives rise up as one to resist the idea.

The institutionalization of the Queens College–Louis Armstrong Middle School collaboration has come from the steady presence of a core group of professors, from the school's success, and from strong constituency support. Still, no matter how long the presence, one cannot evade a key question: How long should we stay?

Despite the fact that the collaboration has functioned for so long, we feel it is necessary to add that such efforts cannot be expected to continue indefinitely and that there may come a time when they should be brought to a conclusion. It is impossible to determine in advance for any project when that time should be. The length of a collaboration's life will vary depending on local circumstances, the personnel involved, the level of available support, the attitude of top leadership, and other similar factors. One clear sign is that if a relationship stops being truly collaborative, then the right move is to end it. The decision to conclude a collaborative relationship is a delicate one, and can be problematic. As with many situations in life, it is easier to begin things than bring them to successful conclusions. Bringing closure to long-term relationships can always result in misunderstandings. The decision needs to be given serious attention and be supported by good long-term planning and preparation.

Question 5: What Has Been the Chief Source of Frustration in Working in the Collaboration?

We have noted earlier the high rate of turnover of those in leadership positions. The need to establish relationships over and over again has been our major frustration. The personality and leadership style of each new administrator has put us in the position of having continually to clarify and assess our role in the collaboration. With the succession of new principals we have experienced a whole range of feelings. With some there has been an easy, exciting exchange of thought. With other principals who were unsure of their role, there was enormous dependency on college input. With other administrators uninclined to share decisions, we have dealt with a sense of being superfluous; in this case, the struggle to maintain a voice in the workings of the school causes particular frustration since we have been accustomed to influencing school decisions.

The result of all the personnel changes is a collaboration in constant flux, and a need for us as leaders of the project to reach beyond the frustration to find additional sources of energy.

Project funding comes from the Central Board of Education. With each change of personnel at the central headquarters there has arisen a need to review for newcomers the history of the collaboration, its inception, its basis in a legal decision, the role of the college, and its philosophical roots as described in the original design. With every shift in the Board of Education bureaucracy, we, as the senior participants in the collaboration, have been obliged to describe and justify the existence of the collaboration. There is considerable frustration in having to repeatedly go over the same territory.

The fact that each succeeding central administration is oblivious to what has previously been started and accomplished results in the late assignment of funds needed to run the project. Often funding is delayed until the summer prior to the beginning of the school year. This leaves the scheduling of college faculty to the project in a questionable state, since professors' programs for the fall semester are formulated in early spring. Each year uncertainty prevails, as both public school and college staff wonder if the collaboration will continue. Such lack of clarity hardly produces equanimity and gets in the way of thoughtful planning.

Educational priorities change as leadership changes. With the appointment of a new principal and the retirement of professors who were arts advocates, the school's emphasis on art, music, and dance has been lost. This has left us with the problem of retrieving what we believe is an essential part of effective middle school education. Part of our ongoing task has been to maintain what has already been achieved and, at the same time, to work for continued progress. This double-pronged effort sometimes brings feelings of weariness.

The New York City school system is characterized by periodic crisis. The collaboration gets caught up in the undercurrent of emergency situations without warning; for example, additional classes of children are mandated to occupy the nooks and crannies of the school building to alleviate a crowded situation in another district. This is done with no consideration of the impact on the existing program. Constantly we need to make recourse to our powers of adaptability.

A great deal of frustration results from feelings that leadership neither understands nor recognizes the achievements of the collaboration. One copes with such feelings by redoubling efforts to engage in activities that are rich with promise for the future — but there can be little doubt that the depth of these frustrations are major obstacles to both the success and continuation of such projects.

Question 6: What Have Been Our Sources of Gratification?

In the early years there was a group of seven professors, plus the dean of the school of education, who met regularly to discuss the progress of the collaboration. This sharing of thinking provided nourishment for the psyche. It was exhilarating to look at the process of change, to consider strategies for initiating new approaches, and to analyze our interaction with the various personalities. It was as if we mutually agreed that life in schools is worth examining. Our numbers have dwindled since the beginning, but we still value those times when we meet to give each other the benefit of our different views.

The collaboration has helped us to overcome campus isolation, a malaise common to many professors. One faculty member put it this way: "I think college professors are even more isolated than public school teachers. You come to the campus, teach your class, and then leave. You never know if you're having any impact. In the collaboration I feel connected to the real world. I have a chance to interact with people in ways that show results. I've been able to work with people I like."

The collaboration has also given us pride of ownership. At the college, activities remain discrete from each other with little connection between subdivisions of the school of education. In the collaboration, we refer to the Louis Armstrong Middle School as "our school." We feel pride in its accomplishments and take pleasure from our interaction with parents, students, teachers, and administrators. We feel connected to this active world and have helped to develop effective educational approaches for 10- to 14-year-olds. We believe that we have made a difference.

Question 7: What Would We Say to Others Considering the Implementation of a School-College Collaboration?

Over two decades our experience has taught us many lessons. When we began, we gave little attention to the reception we might encounter. Nor did we have a clear view of our goals other than to indicate our desire to improve middle school education. We didn't even pause to consider the resources we had available to support our project. We simply blundered ahead, oblivious of the obstacles that might develop. The ambiguity that was present when we started had its advantages as well as its drawbacks. As has been stated previously, the collaboration's lack of specificity allowed us to maintain our idealistic notions regarding what we would like to achieve without being held back by preconceived restraints. But, in retrospect, there are insights, caveats, and precautions worth considering as one prepares to launch a collaboration.

Even before setting forth on a collaborative venture, check out the circumstances surrounding the proposal. What stimulated its inception? Is the college being brought in with some overblown expectations about the level of expertise it can bring to bear on problems? Is the college really wanted by teachers, parents, and administrators as a partner in the collaboration? What monetary and personnel resources will be available? What is college leadership's level of interest in the collaboration, and will the system for promotion reward effort in the field? What are the parameters of time that have been established? Is particular achievement expected in a short period?

Prior thinking about these questions can help prepare for the problems and obstacles that may be encountered, and give a clearer idea of the support that will be available. The responses to these inquiries might also conceivably lead to a decision not to enter into a collaboration. If, for example, the prospect of college involvement is not welcomed by administrators, teachers, and parents or if campus administration evinces only lukewarm support, then the invitation to join forces might better be refused.

Before committing to the collaboration, consideration should be given to how self-interest will be served. Find out if the efforts of you and your colleagues will influence tenure and promotion decisions. Recruit other professors, choosing not only those faculty with skills in working in the field but also those with whom you can share the excitement of exploring new ideas. The resistance to change and the frustration inherent in working with bureaucracy need to be balanced by opportunities for professors to be nurtured through sharing the results of their experience with one another. Consider also if there is a realistic possibility of impacting the schools with which you will be working or whether administration is so negative and the teaching so inadequate, that progress, no matter what the effort, is unlikely.

In addition, it can be useful to think about what reaction you can expect from public school staff. Doing so may soften the response to problems that will arise. For example, be prepared for initial hostility and/ or skepticism on the part of the public school staff. Such feelings are not altogether surprising if we look at the negative history of school–college interaction, and with this in mind it makes establishing positive relationships a priority. A first step toward achieving open acceptance occurs when college personnel enter the school arena not as abstract theoreticians but rather as fellow practitioners offering concrete support. Such support may take the form of needed supplies, acting as teacher advocates, or simply serving as sympathetic listeners.

We have found other approaches that have contributed to the college's acceptance as full partners in the collaboration. They include college personnel becoming a presence in the building and being part of every aspect of school functioning. Professors join curriculum meetings, attend Parents' Association evenings, serve as members of the administrative cabinet, and participate on the school-based management team. They also come together with school staff at such informal occasions as parties, parent–teacher dinner dances, and student–faculty basketball and softball games. We have also seen the importance of keeping leadership informed and involved with college activity. Periodic written reports have proved useful, but even more valuable have been the many face-to-face conversations where ideas and observations have been shared.

It is also necessary to recognize the qualities needed to maintain forward momentum. Patience and persistence are needed in large quantities, for the task of affecting attitudes, developing relationships with ever-changing personnel, and establishing a process that challenges the status quo is formidable. One must be prepared to deal with the discomfort of uncertainty and to be flexible, since unanticipated events will occur causing disruption. The job of developing a collaboration cannot be blueprinted in advance. It is rather a creative enterprise, much like what the artist does. The artist approaches a canvas, thinks about nuances of light and shadow, combinations of color, and the quality of paints. The collaborator, too, has to think of subtle questions — how to apply influence, when to introduce a new idea, how to be critical and yet empathic, how to deal with different persons, personalities, or ego needs, and how to deal with mistakes. The questions never end. Despite the difficulties, school–college collaborations can provide the opportunity to integrate the best of two cultures, to build different structures, and to add a vitality to public schools and to teacher education programs that has been lacking.

For those involved in such efforts, there is an urgent need to maintain a balanced perspective regarding what can be done, how soon it can be accomplished, and what results can realistically be expected. It is important to adopt an attitude that recognizes there are no final answers, there are only approximations and even these fit only for a time. Schools by their very nature are a work in progress, never a finished product. We used the collaboratives process as a means of sharing ideas, insight, and experience, always trying to understand that these have to be consistently adapted to local, individual circumstances. John McDermott (1987), writing on the topic of experience, makes a good case for the type of perspective that is needed:

> Neither optimism nor pessimism are the proper empirical response to the actual situation of the human condition. To be optimistic is to be potentially naive about the vagaries of natural forces which often presage disaster. It is also to be blithely unaware of the human capacity to act in a self-aggrandizing manner, even at the expense of the community or of those values which most of us cherish. On the other hand, to be systematically pessimistic is to draw the curtain on possibility, on growth, on novelty, and on the most indomitable characteristic of the human spirit, the ability to begin again, afresh, with the hope for a better day. (p. 118)

This hope of a better day is the driving force beyond such endeavors.

References

Boyer, E. (1983). *High school*. New York: Harper and Row.

Byrd, V. (1993, August 1). America's schools are not alone. *New York Times Educational Supplement*, section 4A, p. 6.

Carnegie Forum on Education and the Economy. (1986). *A nation prepared: Teachers for the 21st century*. New York: Carnegie Foundation.

Corvasce, F., & Zarnowski, M. (1993). *Life songs: Teaching and learning history in the middle school* (Valuing Diversity Series, Vol. 2, No. 2). New York: Center for the Improvement of Education, Queens College.

Curcio, F., Perez, R., & Stewart, B. (1994). Partnership in mathematics education: The evolution of a professional development school. In D. B. Aichele (Ed.), *Professional development for teachers of mathematics: 1994 yearbook* (pp. 204–213). Reston, VA: National Council of Teachers of Mathematics.

Garfarth, F. (Ed.). (1971). *John Stuart Mill on education*. New York: Teachers College Press.

Goodlad, J. I. (1994). *Educational renewal: Better teachers, better schools*. San Francisco: Jossey-Bass.

Guy, R. (1973). *The friends*. New York: Holt.

Johnson, L., & Smith, S. (1993). *Dealing with diversity through multicultural fiction: Library–classroom partnerships*. Chicago: American Library Association.

Lewis, A. (1990). *Making it in the middle: The how and why of excellent schools for young urban adolescents*. New York: Edna McConnell Clark Foundation.

Maeroff, G. (1983). *School and college: partnerships in education*. Princeton, NJ: Princeton University Press.

McDermott, J. (1987). *Streams of experience: Reflections on the history and philosophy of American culture*. Amherst: University of Massachusetts Press.

Muncey, D., & McQuillan, P. (1993, February). Preliminary findings from a five-year study of the Coalition of Essential Schools. *Phi Delta Kappan, 74*(6), 486–489.

National Commission on Excellence in Education. (1983). *A nation at risk*. Washington, DC: National Commission on Excellence in Education.

Sarason, S. (1971). *The culture of the school and the problem of change*. Boston: Allyn and Bacon.

Sarason, S. (1995). *School change: The personal development of a point of view*. New York: Teachers College Press.

Schlesinger, J. (1994, February 28). The talk of the town. *The New Yorker, 70*(2), p. 42.

Tobier, A. (1992). *Just trying to live and sweet concordia: Two oral histories taken down and edited by Arthur Tobier.* New York: Center for the Improvement of Education, Queens College/City University of New York.

Trubowitz, S. (1986). Stages in the development of school–college collaboration. *Educational Leadership*, 43, 18–21.

Trubowitz, S. (1994). The quest for the good advisor–advisee program. *Middle Ground* (Winter), 3–5.

Trubowitz, S., Duncan, J., Fibkins, W., Longo, P., & Sarason, S. (1984). *When a college works with a public school.* Boston: Institute for Responsive Education.

Index

About the Authors

Dr. Sidney Trubowitz has been a teacher, school administrator, professor of educational administration, chairperson of the Department of Graduate Programs, and Associate Dean of Education at the Queens College School of Education. He headed up the School's Center for the Improvement of Education with its network of schools involved in middle level education. More recently, he has returned to his position as Director of the Queens College program at the Louis Armstrong Middle School. One of his publications, *A Handbook for Teaching at the Ghetto School*, was a direct result of his years as assistant principal and principal in Harlem elementary schools. His articles have appeared in such periodicals as *Phi Delta Kappan*, *Educational Leadership*, *Urban Education*, and *The Principal*.

Prior to returning to Louis Armstrong and Queens College in 1991, he served as executive director of the Westchester School Partnership at the State University of New York at Purchase. In that capacity, he coordinated staff development activity for 33 school districts associated with the college.

Dr. Paul Longo spent his first eleven years in education working in four different school districts, serving nine years as a classroom teacher and the last two as an administrator. Since that time, he has been employed at Queens College, where he has occupied a number of roles.

He began his career at the college teaching method of mathematics and science in the Department of Elementary and Early Childhood Education. During that time he maintained contact with the public schools through his work as a student teaching supervisor, but primarily through his role as an evaluator of Title I programs and curriculum consultant. Eventually, Dr. Longo served in a number of administrative posts, including Coordinator of Student Teaching, Director of Educational Placement, department chair, and Associate Dean of the School of Education. His present position is Director of the Center for the Improvement of Education. Apart from his evaluations, Dr. Longo has published articles in a number of journals including *Educational Forum*, *Phi Delta Kappan*, *School and Community*, and *Educational Leadership*.